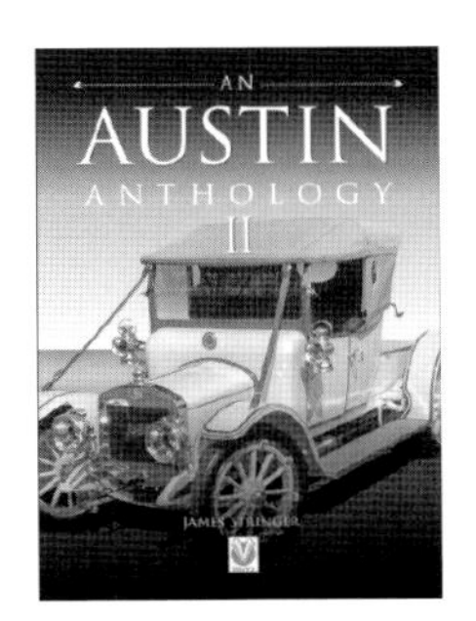
AN
AUSTIN
ANTHOLOGY
II

Also from Veloce:

Those Were The Days ... Series
Alpine Trials & Rallies 1910-1973 (Pfundner)
American 'Independent' Automakers – AMC to Willys 1945 to 1960 (Mort)
American Station Wagons – The Golden Era 1950-1975 (Mort)
American Woodies 1928-1953 (Mort)
Anglo-American Cars from the 1930s to the 1970s (Mort)
Austerity Motoring (Bobbitt)
Austins, The last real (Peck)
Brighton National Speed Trials (Gardiner)
British Touring Car Racing (Collins)
British Woodies (Peck)
Don Hayter's MGB Story – The birth of the MGB in MG's Abingdon Design & Development Office (Hayter)
MG's Abingdon Factory (Moylan)
Three Wheelers (Bobbitt)

Great Cars
Austin-Healey – A celebration of the fabulous 'Big' Healey (Piggott)
Jaguar E-type (Thorley)
Jaguar Mark 1 & 2 (Thorley)
Jaguar XK A Celebration of Jaguar's 1950s Classic (Thorley)
Triumph TR – TR2 to 6: The last of the traditional sports cars (Piggott)
Volkswagen Beetle – A Celebration of the World's Most Popular Car (Copping)

Biographies
A Life Awheel – The 'auto' biography of W de Forte (Skelton)
Amédée Gordini ... a true racing legend (Smith)
André Lefebvre, and the cars he created at Voisin and Citroën (Beck)
Bunty – Remembering a gentleman of noble Scottish-Irish descent (Schrader)
Cliff Allison, The Official Biography of – From the Fells to Ferrari (Gauld)
Driven by Desire – The Desiré Wilson Story
First Principles – The Official Biography of Keith Duckworth (Burr)
Inspired to Design – F1 cars, Indycars & racing tyres: the autobiography of Nigel Bennett (Bennett)
Jack Sears, The Official Biography of – Gentleman Jack (Gauld)
John Chatham – 'Mr Big Healey' – The Official Biography (Burr)
The Lee Noble Story (Wilkins)
Raymond Mays' Magnificent Obsession (Apps)
Pat Moss Carlsson Story, The – Harnessing Horsepower (Turner)
Tony Robinson – The biography of a race mechanic (Wagstaff)
Virgil Exner – Visioneer: The Official Biography of Virgil M Exner Designer Extraordinaire (Grist)

General
AC Two-litre Saloons & Buckland Sportscars (Archibald)
Alfa Romeo Montreal – The dream car that came true (Taylor)
Alfa Romeo Montreal – The Essential Companion (Classic Reprint of 500 copies) (Taylor)
Alfa Tipo 33 (McDonough & Collins)
Alpine & Renault – The Sports Prototypes 1963 to 1969 (Smith)
Alpine & Renault – The Sports Prototypes 1973 to 1978 (Smith)
An Austin Anthology (Stringer)
An Incredible Journey (Falls & Reisch)
Anatomy of the Classic Mini (Huthert & Ely)
Anatomy of the Works Minis (Moylan)
Armstrong-Siddeley (Smith)
Art Deco and British Car Design (Down)
Austin Cars 1948 to 1990 – A Pictorial History (Rowe)
Autodrome (Collins & Ireland)
Automotive A-Z, Lane's Dictionary of Automotive Terms (Lane)
Automotive Mascots (Kay & Springate)
Bahamas Speed Weeks, The (O'Neil)
Bentley Continental, Corniche and Azure (Bennett)
Bentley MkVI, Rolls-Royce Silver Wraith, Dawn & Cloud/Bentley R & S-Series (Nutland)
Bluebird CN7 (Stevens)
British at Indianapolis, The (Wagstaff)
British Cars, The Complete Catalogue of, 1895-1975 (Culshaw & Horrobin)
Bugatti – The eight-cylinder Touring Cars 1920-34 (Price & Arbey)
Carrera Panamericana, La (Tipler)
Chevrolet Corvette (Starkey)
Chrysler 300 – America's Most Powerful Car 2nd Edition (Ackerson)
Chrysler PT Cruiser (Ackerson)
Citroën DS (Bobbitt)
Classic British Car Electrical Systems (Astley)
Cobra – The Real Thing! (Legate)
Concept Cars, How to illustrate and design – New 2nd Edition (Dewey)
Cortina – Ford's Bestseller (Robson)
Cosworth – The Search for Power (6th edition) (Robson)
Coventry Climax Racing Engines (Hammill)
Daimler SP250 New Edition (Long)
Datsun Fairlady Roadster to 280ZX – The Z-Car Story (Long)
Dino – The V6 Ferrari (Long)
Dorset from the Sea – The Jurassic Coast from Lyme Regis to Old Harry Rocks photographed from its best viewpoint (also Souvenir Edition) (Belasco)
Draw & Paint Cars – How to (Gardiner)
Drive on the Wild Side, A – 20 Extreme Driving Adventures From Around the World (Weaver)
East German Motor Vehicles in Pictures (Suhr/Weinreich)
Essential Guide to Driving in Europe, The (Parish)
Fast Ladies – Female Racing Drivers 1888 to 1970 (Bouzanquet)
Fate of the Sleeping Beauties, The (op de Weegh/Hottendorff/op de Weegh)
Ford Midsize Muscle – Fairlane, Torino & Ranchero (Cranswick)
Ford Model Y (Roberts)
France: the essential guide for car enthusiasts – 200 things for the car enthusiast to see and do (Parish)
Immortal Austin Seven (Morgan)
India - The Shimmering Dream (Reisch/Falls (translator)
Intermeccanica – The Story of the Prancing Bull (McCredie & Reisner)
Jaguar, The Rise of (Price)
Jeep CJ (Ackerson)
The Jowett Jupiter – The car that leaped to fame (Nankivell)
Karmann-Ghia Coupé & Convertible (Bobbitt)
Lancia 037 (Collins)
Lancia Delta HF Integrale (Blaettel & Wagner)
Lancia Delta Integrale (Collins)
Land Rover Design - 70 years of success (Hull)
Land Rover, The Half-ton Military (Cook)
Lea-Francis Story, The (Price)
Le Mans Panoramic (Ireland)
Lexus Story, The (Long)
Lola – The Illustrated History (1957-1977) (Starkey)
Lola – All the Sports Racing & Single-seater Racing Cars 1978-1997 (Starkey)
Lotus 18 Colin Chapman's U-turn (Whitelock)
Lotus 49 (Oliver)
Making a Morgan (Hensing)
Mazda Rotary-engined Cars (Cranswick)
Maximum Mini (Booij)
Meet the English (Bowie)
MG, Made in Abingdon (Frampton)
MGA (Price Williams)
MGB & MGB GT– Expert Guide (Auto-doc Series) (Williams)
MGB – The Illustrated History, Updated Fourth Edition (Wood & Burrell)
Mini Cooper – The Real Thing! (Tipler)
Mini Minor to Asia Minor (West)
Mitsubishi Lancer Evo, The Road Car & WRC Story (Long)
Montlhéry, The Story of the Paris Autodrome (Boddy)
MOPAR Muscle – Barracuda, Dart & Valiant 1960-1980 (Cranswick)
Morgan Maverick (Lawrence)
Morgan 3 Wheeler – back to the future!, The (Dron)
Morris Minor, 70 Years on the Road (Newell)
Motor Movies – The Posters! (Veysey)
Motor Racing – Reflections of a Lost Era (Carter)
Motor Racing – The Pursuit of Victory 1930-1962 (Carter)
Motor Racing – The Pursuit of Victory 1963-1972 (Wyatt/Sears)
Motor Racing Heroes – The Stories of 100 Greats (Newman)
Motorsport In colour, 1950s (Wainwright)
MV Agusta Fours, The book of the classic (Falloon)
Nissan 300ZX & 350Z – The Z-Car Story (Long)
Northeast American Sports Car Races 1950-1959 (O'Neil)
Norton Commando Bible – All models 1968 to 1978 (Henshaw)
Nothing Runs – Misadventures in the Classic, Collectable & Exotic Car Biz (Slutsky)
Patina Volkswagens (Walker)
Pontiac Firebird – New 3rd Edition (Cranswick)
Racing Colours – Motor Racing Compositions 1908-2009 (Newman)
Roads with a View – England's greatest views and how to find them by road (Corfield)
Rolls-Royce Silver Shadow/Bentley T Series Corniche & Camargue – Revised & Enlarged Edition (Bobbitt)
Rolls-Royce Silver Spirit, Silver Spur & Bentley Mulsanne 2nd Edition (Bobbitt)
Rootes Cars of the 50s, 60s & 70s – Hillman, Humber, Singer, Sunbeam & Talbot, A Pictorial History (Rowe)
Rover Cars 1945 to 2005, A Pictorial History
Runways & Racers (O'Neil)
Russian Motor Vehicles – Soviet Limousines 1930-2003 (Kelly)
Russian Motor Vehicles – The Czarist Period 1784 to 1917 (Kelly)
Schlumpf – The intrigue behind the most beautiful car collection in the world (Op de Weegh & Op de Weegh)
Sleeping Beauties USA – abandoned classic cars & trucks (Marek)
Speedway – Auto racing's ghost tracks (Collins & Ireland)
Standard Motor Company, The Book of the (Robson)
Tales from the Toolbox (Oliver)
Tatra – The Legacy of Hans Ledwinka, Updated & Enlarged Collector's Edition of 1500 copies (Margolius & Henry)
This Day in Automotive History (Corey)
To Boldly Go – twenty six vehicle designs that dared to be different (Hull)
Triumph & Standard Cars 1945 to 1984 (Warrington)
Triumph Bonneville!, Save the – The inside story of the Meriden Workers' Co-op (Rosamond)
Volkswagens of the World (Glen)
Which Oil? – Choosing the right oils & greases for your antique, vintage, veteran, classic or collector car (Michell)
Wolseley Cars 1948 to 1975 (Rowe)
Works MGs, The (Allison & Browning)
Works Minis, The Last (Purves & Brenchley)
Works Rally Mechanic (Moylan)

www.veloce.co.uk

First published in March 2019 by Veloce Publishing Limited, Veloce House, Parkway Farm Business Park, Middle Farm Way, Poundbury, Dorchester DT1 3AR, England. Tel +44 (0)1305 260068 / Fax 01305 250479 / e-mail info@veloce.co.uk / web www.veloce.co.uk or www.velocebooks.com. ISBN: 978-1-787114-26-5; UPC: 6-36847-01426-1.

Readers with ideas for automotive books, or books on other transport or related hobby subjects, are invited to write to the editorial director of Veloce Publishing at the above address. British Library Cataloguing in Publication Data – A catalogue record for this book is available from the British Library. Typesetting, design and page make-up all by Veloce Publishing Ltd on Apple Mac. Printed in India by Replika Press.

AN

AUSTIN ANTHOLOGY II

JAMES STRINGER

CONTENTS

DEDICATION

I dedicate this book to my wife, Avril, my son, Andrew, and my daughter, Johanna, and also to my four grandchildren, Luke, Tom, Molly and Katie.

Publisher's note
Illustrating a book of this type is a real challenge, as many of the images supporting the text are of poor quality. However, we make no apologies for the inclusion of such images as they are of immeasurable importance in terms of enhancing these stories from the past.

Foreword

by Norman John Milne

Ex-Austin man, fellow archivist & BMC historian

An ex-Longbridge chum, who is chairman of one of the many Austin owners' and supporters' clubs around the world, wrote once: "I wonder what we'll do when we run out of Austin stories." I retorted sharply in print: "We'll never manage to exhaust fascinating Austin and Longbridge 'family' sagas ..."

Certainly Jim Stringer has seen to that. Pillar of the Austin firmament worldwide, stalwart of the longstanding Vintage Austin Register, revered author and encyclopaedic editor of the *Vintage Austin Magazine* over more than 50 years, Jim knows as much about Austin cars, taxis, boats, aeroplanes and Austin folk as anyone.

As he knows more than most about the testing tales that were never published, or incredible stories long forgotten ...

Take the first of his new books: *An Austin Anthology* published in 2018. A score of truly riveting tales (without giving too much away) exercises his insight into topics as wide ranging as: Lord Austin's little-known younger brother; an 'affordable' biplane you could keep in your garage; the world's very first motor home; ghastly murder within the Austin Village; circus-clowning and war work for the million-mile London taxis!

Now we welcome another Stringer Anthology, as unique, as revealing, and as thought-provoking as the first. 22 more exposés of topics like: The mischief that Herbert Austin's youngest daughter got up to; what Austin engineers did to ensure that the world's fastest racing boat did win; a Swift peep into the first Austin Seven; why Austin armoured Cars had to be sent to Russia; how cartoonists portrayed the truly Baby Austin; or would you prefer to know what Adolf Hitler said to Austin at the Berlin Motor Show?

All will be revealed in this fascinating book.

Whatever your interest or priorities, Jim here has plenty to stimulate and intrigue you through his writing and research. Along with others devoted to the heritage and highlights of Austin – Bob Wyatt, Zita Lambert, Barney Sharratt, to mention but a few – Stringer is a giant of the genre. He loves telling stories.

By comparison, my offerings are modest. Through spending 12 instructive, memorable years with Austin at Longbridge, and more than 30 in the Motor Industry, a claim about three million words devoted to Austin is all I can justify – and that's largely due to old age! Share, absorb and enjoy Jim's enthusiasms.

NORMAN JOHN MILNE

Introduction

ABOUT THE AUTHOR

Jim Stringer

I was born in Shepherd's Bush in the January of 1943, during the time when the Luftwaffe was busy carrying out yet another bombing raid on London. Brought home from the hospital a week or so later through the debris strewn streets of West London in the comfort and safety of a 1935 Austin Taxicab with coachwork by Jones Bros' of Westbourne Grove, and thus commenced an instant affection for all things 'Austin.' The taxicab, which explains how I knew so much about it, was of course owned by a neighbour who, in later years would kindly bring me home from school in it!

When old enough to drive, and much to my father's dismay, I purchased a 1929 Austin 16/6 saloon car with rare 'fabric' coachwork. A relationship which was not improved upon when, despite being told not to put the car in the garage where I lived, as it was likely to drip oil on the floor, I defied my father and almost destroyed the doors at the far end of it when putting the car away for the first time, having depressed the 'accelerator' pedal instead of the 'brake.' It was interesting to note that my three friends and colleagues who insisted that the car be 'garaged,' and helped by guiding it into the forbidden garage, left for home very quickly without saying 'goodbye.' That same Austin still holds pride of place in the 'Stringer' household even to this day.

On purchasing the Austin for the princely sum of £35, I then became a member of the Vintage Austin Register, and very soon became involved in its organisation, from initially helping with the first Newsletter, to becoming the Hon. Sec., then Chairman. I then 'retired,' but two years later took on the job of producing the Register's glossy quarterly magazine as its editor. But not content with waiting for 'contributions' to be sent in by its members I started to undertake research into many hitherto untold stories concerning Austin vehicles and aeroplanes and of course the people who purchased them, drove them, flew them or were simply involved in their manufacture.

The author's 1929 Austin 16/6 'fabric' saloon.

In this second anthology I have included a further 22 stories which, like those in my previous book, have never been thoroughly researched or published before.

I am a life member of the Vintage Austin Register, and also Vice President, and after an absence of six years came out of retirement once again to act as (caretaker) editor for the VAR's quarterly journal again until such time as a new editor could be found. Which thankfully has since occurred.

INTRODUCTION TO THE BOOK

In my previous book, *An Austin Anthology* I aimed to provide the reader with a wider understanding of the important role The Austin Motor Company played in the development of the motor car, and how, through the engineering skills of Herbert Austin and his team of designers, engineers and craftsmen he was able to manufacture motor cars which not only were 'right' at the time but which have since stood the test of time by out-living many of their contemporaries which is shown through their remarkable survival rate today.

This may be aptly illustrated when viewing period television dramas set in the 1920s and 1930s. The most commonly noted vehicles either to be seen as a principle car or just being used as 'dressing' or 'traffic' will most likely to be an Austin. I was once asked why it was that Austins were most prominent, as seen, for example, in the Poirot series of stories. My answer was simply that because they were well designed and well built, their survival rate has exceeded that of most of their contemporaries, and therefore there were more Austin motor cars and taxicabs available for such roles than, say, for example, Morris or Fords.

In *An Austin Anthology* I covered many hitherto untold stories of Austin motor cars and aeroplanes, often carrying out considerable research into why they should be of interest to today's motorists and enthusiasts. In this book I have unearthed 22 additional tales with which to illustrate why the Austin name still remains of some significance even today and should therefore never be forgotten, and as 'research' never stops, Chapter 22 includes a couple more snippets which have come to light since the previous book was published.

In the first chapter I have taken a long hard look at how Herbert Austin managed to produce a new motor car from scratch in only a few months after establishing his Company at Longbridge. I have also taken an in depth look at the 100 horse power Austins which were built for, and raced in the French Grand Prix at Dieppe in 1908, and then traced what happened to them afterwards. I have also covered the request for armoured cars for use by the Imperial Russian Army in 1914, and also the very first Austin Seven designed as a single cylinder two seater voiturette, and which was also marketed as, and also manufactured alongside a 7hp Swift!

Each chapter in this Anthology represents but a small piece of our motoring history, which although not warranting an entire book to be devoted to each story, sits comfortably within the pages of this second compendium, and in doing so brings to the reader a broader knowledge of 'The Austin.'

JAMES (JIM) STRINGER

Acknowledgements

In compiling this work which covers a few of the lesser-known activities of the Austin Motor Company, its products and those who had experience with them, I found it sometimes necessary to consult the works of others who have previously touched upon the same subjects. Where the authors of such research is known, their work in this respect is gratefully acknowledged.

The first chapter owes much to the original research carried out by the late Ross Haynes. Mike Eggenton of the VAR contributed much to the story about Adolf Hitler and his 'Dixi.' The Zita Austin story was reproduced courtesy of the *Birmingham Evening Post*. The photograph of Prideaux Garage was sent to me from David Waller of the Dorset Austin Seven Club, and comes with acknowledgement to the publication *Glimpses of the Past – Lynton and Lynmouth* by John Travis (ISBN-10: 1859830862).

Driving Miss Daisy was the work of Martin Woodward, and just had to be included as originally written. The chapter on Alf Depper was taken from the transcript of an interview recorded in 1967 by Barry Quann of the *BMC World* magazine.

The cartoons featured in *Funny little Austin Sevens* came from various sources, but mainly from within the pages of the *Austin Magazine* & *Austin Advocate*. The information on the two Austin Seven songs again came from various sources including the VAR Archive. The 100hp Austins were originally researched by the late Ross Haynes. With additional and significant input from Barry Davies. No.45 was sourced from the *Austin Advocate* magazine as was the account on Felix Scriven's Sergeant Murphy with photographs supplied by Mike Worthington-Williams. The story behind Maple Leaf IV was also inspired by a report published in the *Austin Advocate* magazine.

Information and photographs on the Austin Armoured cars came from the author's own collection, the *Austin Advocate* magazine and from the highly informative website edited by Michael Delera, the Maythorne Austin Seven was inspired by a piece written in the *Austin Magazine* and the recent photograph with kind acknowledgement to Bonhams, the Auctioneers.

Additional information on the 40hp motor home and 'Pobble' (see previous book) came from papers supplied by Ian Dimmer. Information concerning the first Austin Seven came from various sources, but Norman Milne provided the transcript of the testing of the one preserved in Gaydon, whilst extracts from the owner's diary were first published by Anthony Bird in the *Veteran & Vintage Magazine* in 1972.

JAMES (JIM) STRINGER

Chapter 1

Was the first Austin actually an Austin?

This is a question which has been asked many times over the years, with very strong suggestions that it may actually have been a Gladiator, which was, in fact, a French motor car.

The mystery deepens further when, back in the 1920s, both Herbert Austin and Harvey Du Cros jnr were asked that very same question by Dudley Maddick from *The Sporting and Dramatic News*, who, at that time, owned an 18/24 Austin Gladiator. Both Du Cros and Austin were very evasive, and neither provided the answer that would, undoubtedly, have put the matter to rest once and for all.

In this chapter I will endeavour to provide as much information as is known about the early days of The Austin Motor Company, the vehicle in question, and about those who were there at the time, and leave the reader to make up his or her own mind as to what the answer may be.

Herbert Austin fell out with the Vickers brothers over a dispute as to what type of engine should be installed in their new generation of motor vehicles. Albert and Thomas Vickers wanted to ditch the two-cylinder horizontally-opposed engines (which, up until then, had powered their current range of motor vehicles) in favour of the more conventional vertical four-cylinder engines, which were, by now, beginning to be used in most other makes of motor car. Austin was very much against this and he dug his heels in, and, because of his firmly held views on this matter, he was finally forced to part company with Wolseley. However, the actual reason for Herbert Austin's departure was that he was seen to be spending far too much time away from his desk, mainly abroad, and not spending enough time on his work with Wolseley. Austin was advised of their decision on his return from France, and when told, he departed once more across the channel. It may, of course, be assumed that his frequent trips to France could well have been to visit the premises of Clement-Gladiator, but we will never know.

At the relatively young age of 38, it was possibly the break that he was looking for, as he had always harboured ambitions of starting up his own motor car manufacturing company, and, even before his departure, he was actively seeking suitable premises in which this could be established.

On 4th November, he discovered an empty factory on the outskirts of Birmingham, in a village called Longbridge. The premises were only a few years old and had previously been occupied by a company of tinplate printers called White & Pike. The asking price was £10,000, but, after negotiation, he was able to obtain the buildings and surrounding land for just £7750.

On the 17th of that month, two drawings appeared pinned to a board on stand 42 at the London Motor Show presenting the 'New' Austin motor car. The stand was allocated to Harvey Du Cros, who was the sole concessionaire for Mercedes Motors, but the interesting thing was that the drawings were of a conventional, chain driven 18/24hp chassis, into which was mounted a vertical four-cylinder engine – a far cry from those previously produced at Wolseley and which Austin had been so keen to defend.

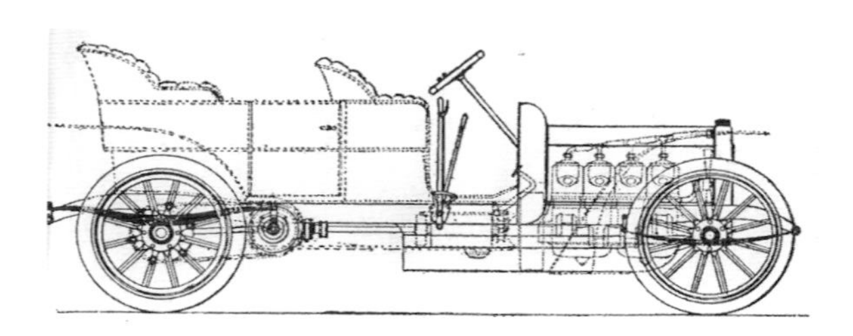

The drawing displayed at Olympia.
(Courtesy Bob Wyatt)

Harvey Du Cros, who had interests in a number of concerns, such as Dunlop Tyres, Mercedes Cars, Swift Cars, Ariel Motor Cars, and Clement-Gladiator, was also one of Herbert Austin's two financial backers. The other was Captain Frank Kayser who owned the Kayser Ellison steel company.

Both of these gentlemen played a very important role in establishing the Austin Motor Company in the first few months of its existence and beyond, and perhaps may well have influenced his design for the first Austin to a certain degree. It should also be noted that Harvey Du Cros had his main office in London's Longacre, which also acted as a showroom for the cars in which he had an interest, and which would, of course, have been available to Herbert Austin.

On leaving Wolseley on November 17th, Austin invited a number of his employees to come with him and be part of his new venture, these included Alfred J Hancock (draughtsman), A V Davidge, William (Bobby) Howitt (Private Secretary), and Austin's younger brother,

The premises belonging to Harvey Du Cros in Long Acre, London, from where Austin was able to display his motor cars.
(Courtesy VAR Archive)

Harry. Alfred Hancock was immediately installed at Austin's house in Berwood Grove, Erdington, where he was set to work designing the first Austin motor car.

When Herbert Austin moved into his new premises, on 22nd January 1906, it was, for all intents and purposes, just an empty building. The offices were quite bare and there were no machines, such as lathes or milling machines, in what were to be the workshops. All these and much more not only had to be purchased, but installed too.

It is understood that the machine shop facilities of the Ariel Motor Company, based in Bournbrook, were made available to Austin through Harvey Du Cros. So, for the short term, until such facilities could be established at Longbridge, he was at least able to undertake most of the required engineering tasks.

On February 17th the first advertisement for Austin motor cars appeared in *The Autocar* magazine. It stated: "Success gained in the past by the designer of the Austin Cars: Gold Medals, 16, Silver Medals, 8, For reliability, Speed and Hill Climbing," Whilst these statements were clearly describing Wolseley motor cars, it was certainly intended to impart to the motoring public that it was, in fact, Austin who had gained all these awards.

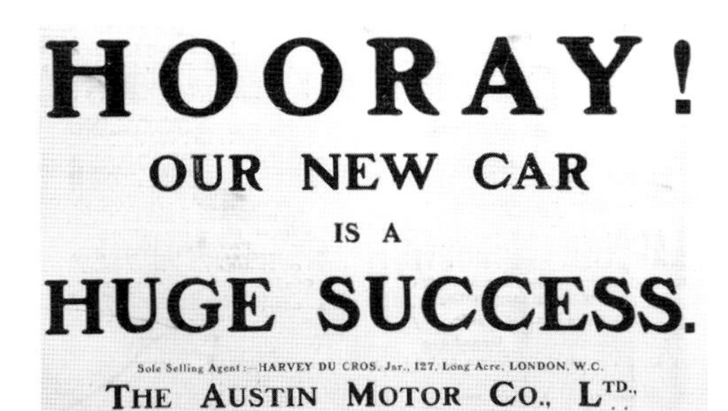

One of the earliest advertisements for Austin Motor Cars.

The initial test run of the first car in late March was not without its problems: over-lubrication, intended to prevent any thoughts the engine may have had with regard to seizing up, showed itself in clouds of blue smoke coming from the exhaust. Leaks, too, from various parts of the engine infuriated an already tense Herbert Austin (which lead to the immediate sacking of two coppersmiths that he considered responsible). However in spite of all this, the test run was considered highly successful, and the two coppersmiths were duly re-instated.

By 26th April, the first Austin Motor car had been completed and was

Herbert Austin (in bowler hat) over-seeing work on the engine of the first Austin (Courtesy VAR archive)

Above: The first Austin completed with touring coachwork. (Courtesy VAR Archive)

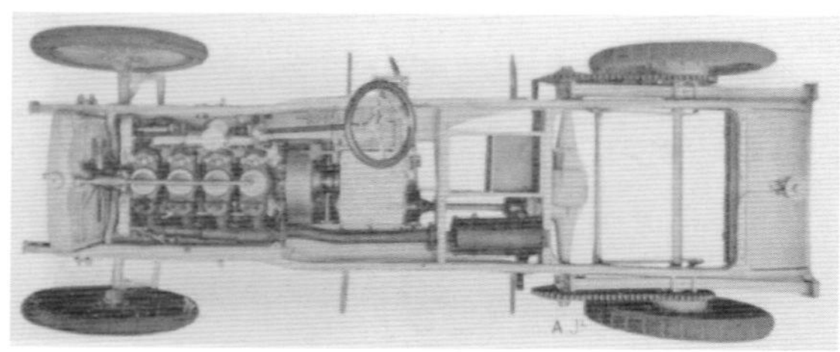

Above: A plan view of the chassis of the first 25/30 hp Austin. (Courtesy VAR Archive)

A front view of the completed chassis of the first Austin.

Rear view of the first chassis.

A view of the nearside of the first Austin chassis.

The first Austin on a trial run within the Longbridge factory. (Courtesy VAR Archive)

Herbert and Helen Austin, together with son, Vernon, sitting in the (unfinished) first Austin motor car.

ready to be demonstrated to the press. It emerged through the gates at Longbridge with a determined looking bowler-hatted Herbert Austin at the wheel, and accompanied by representatives of the press, and selected engineers from the factory; it was driven towards the gates and, following a left turn, headed up the road towards the Lickey Hills.

The event was marked by an elaborate luncheon, which was also timed to celebrate the official opening of the Factory, and which was attended by eighty friends and trade notables. The toast, raised by Herbert Austin, was to the success of the Austin Motor Company.

Contemporary magazines and journals reported on the occasion thus: "Even before Thursday last when we visited the place of their birth on the occasion of the inaugural function connected with the completion of the first Austin car it was a foregone conclusion, with all those who were well acquainted with Mr Austin, that his latest productions would be a credit to his country. And now we are bound to confess that this remarkably successful designer and builder has exceeded the anticipations of his best friends. Unless we are much mistaken his new cars will be able to hold their own with any of those produced either in this country or abroad, for although time must naturally elapse before prolonged experience on the road can give its final confirmation to our views, we have been more than favourably impressed with what we have already seen of Mr Austin's latest achievement" (*The Automotor Journal*). Further on in the same journal we read: "The 25/30hp is that which has been first completed, and it was a chain driven car of this type which was finished off ready for the road last week. Our illustration shows that it has a neat appearance, and that the chassis is admirably adapted to take any form of touring or town body. A trial run proved that it is sufficiently light in relationship to its power to render it extremely flexible and lively even upon heavy roads, and that the suspension is such as to afford most comfortable and easy riding."

The Austin Motor Co. Limited

Luncheon
Given on the occasion of the completion of the first car

MENU·

CLEAR OX TAIL SOUP
MAYONNAISE OF SALMON
PRAWNS IN ASPIC
RAISED FRENCH PIE
ROAST CHICKEN YORK HAM
CHAUDFROID OF PIGEON
FORE QUARTER OF LAMB & MINT SAUCE
BEEF A LA [illegible]
FRENCH SALAD
OX TONGUE
TRIFLE
MACEDOINE OF FRUITS
CHARTREUSE OF APRICOT
COFFEE ÉCLAIRS FRENCH PASTRY
WINE JELLY
DESSERT
BISCUITS, CHEESE ETC
CAFÉ NOIR
LIQUEURS

1895

1906

The luncheon menu given on the occasion of the completion of the first Austin motor car. Note the signatures of Captain Frank Kayser and Herbert Austin.

The Autocar reported that: "The engine ran with great smoothness and sweetness; The Austin car struck me as being exceedingly well designed and workmanlike and an excellent example of the combination of refinement and strength." The report in *The Motor* stated that "Mr

Austin has made a powerful, quiet and flexible motor. Ample strength throughout the mechanism, maximum compactness without the least loss of accessibility." Finally, back to *The Automotor Journal*, which concludes with the following: "A1 British model, which combines, with the widely recognised reliability of Wolseley cars designed by Mr Herbert Austin. The best and most popular features of up-to-date orthodox practice."

Interestingly, the drawing of the first Austin, which had been pinned to a board on the Mercedes stand at the London Motor Show, described it as an 18/24, however *The Automotor Journal* suggested in its article that it was, in fact, a 25/30 model! The first car was described as a 25hp Endcliffe Phaeton and was offered for sale at £650.

In the first years of manufacturing at Longbridge, The Gladiator motor cars were being manufactured in the same factory, alongside the Austin motor cars to which they bore an uncanny resemblance.

And so, as you can deduce from the above evidence, there is, perhaps, quite a strong indication that Herbert Austin may have been influenced by an already well established motor car, which may have formed the basis of his design for the first Austin motor car.

Herbert Austin presented the first fifty buyers of an Austin motor car with a gold pocket watch (or a wrist watch for the ladies), on the back of which was engraved the company's Wings & Wheel trademark which was designed by Austin in a bedroom at his Berwood Grove home.

The gold half-hunter pocket watch given to each of the first fifty purchasers of an Austin motor car.

Chapter 2

"Wo ist mein Dixi?"

"Where is my Dixi?"

The Austin Motor Company was the sole British motor vehicle manufacturer invited to exhibit at the 1935 German Motor Show, which was held in Berlin. Herbert Austin had brought examples of all the latest models to display on the Austin stand, which attracted a considerable amount of interest amongst the visitors.

Herbert Austin attended the opening of the exhibition, which was conducted, with great ceremony, by the führer, Adolf Hitler, who was unashamedly using the exhibition to show the world just how much Germany had progressed under national nocialism since he became its chancellor and leader.

It came as no surprise to Austin when advised that Herr Hitler was intending to pay a visit to the Austin stand, and that he was to be on hand to be introduced to him.

The German Chancellor, Adolf Hitler, being introduced to Sir Herbert Austin when visiting the Austin stand at the 1935 Berlin Motor Show. (Courtesy VAR Archive)

When Hitler arrived, accompanied by Reich Marshall Hermann Göring, Paul Geisler – the Gauleiter of Munich, and Jacob Werlin, who was Chief of German Motor Transport and director of Daimler-Benz AG, it soon became clear that he was particularly interested in the Austin Seven Speedily, an open sports car.

"Where is the Dixi, I cannot see one, where is it?" he asked one of the members on the Austin stand, and, through an interpreter, they explained to him that the Austin Motor Company did not actually manufacture the Dixi. A Dixi was an Austin Seven which was made under licence in Germany by the Bayerische Motoren Werke Company (BMW), who had purchased the Dixi Werks at Eisenach, gaining with it the licence to build them. The Führer made it known that he had great respect for his Dixi, as it was this particular motor car that he had used whilst driving around Germany campaigning for his National Socialist Party; had it not been for his Dixi, he would probably not have been able to travel all over Germany organising rallies and meetings, he said "Without my little car, this great party of ours would not have been the success that it is today."

Adolf Hitler together with Sir Herbert Austin admiring the Austin 7 Speedily at the Austin Stand. (Courtesy VAR Archive)

Adolf Hitler lavished considerable praise upon the Austin motor cars which were exhibited, and, in particular, the Seven. Jacob Werlin was also showing more than just a passing interest in the little car – examining it very closely and making copious notes.

Later that same day, Hitler was to publicly announce his plan to build a 'People's Car' (or Volks Wagen), which was to be designed by Dr Ferdinand Porsche.

The Austin Motor Company was to exhibit at the Berlin Motor Show for at least a further two years, still the only British car manufacturer invited to do so, and, on each occasion, the Austin stand was visited by Herr Hitler.

It is interesting to note that the Austin Seven 'Speedily' seen in the photographs still exists in Germany, and has recently undergone a programme of extensive restoration.

Chapter 3

Licorice sweets collector's cards

Up until the beginning of the Second World War, smokers of most brands of cigarettes would expect to find a small collector's card, commonly known as a 'Cigarette Card,' enclosed within each packet. These small cards were always very informative, and all manner of subjects were covered by them, from the Kings and Queens of England, cricketers, locomotives, birds, flowers and, of course, motor cars.

Two 'typical' cigarette cards from the mid 1920s. The top one is from a set issued by the United Tobacco Company and depicts an Austin 20/4 Limousine. Below it is one featuring the Austin 12/4 Clifton Tourer, which could be found in packets of The Imperial Tobacco Company's *Lambert & Butler's* brand.

Usually sets, such as the ones shown above comprised of fifty cards, and small albums in which to keep them, could be purchased for just a few pennies.

However, on the other side of the world, a Melbourne-based sweet manufacturer, *Giant Brand Licorice Sweets,* was including its own version of collector cards, one of which could be found in each pack of its licorice sweets.

Collector card number 'A8' features a 1929 Austin 16/6, with Australian-built coachwork.

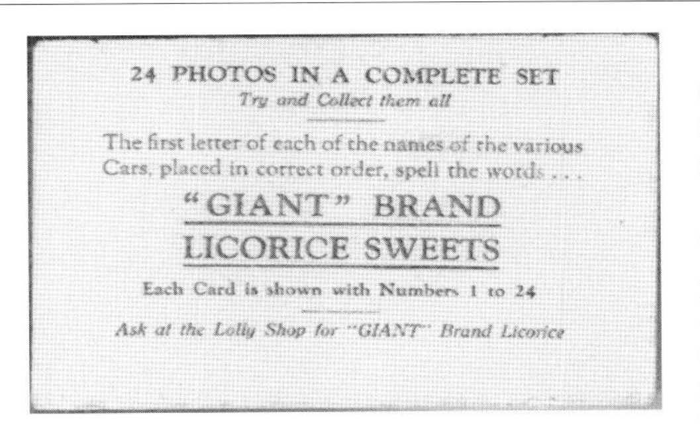
24 PHOTOS IN A COMPLETE SET
Try and Collect them all

The first letter of each of the names of the various Cars, placed in correct order, spell the words . . .

"GIANT" BRAND
LICORICE SWEETS

Each Card is shown with Numbers 1 to 24

Ask at the Lolly Shop for "GIANT" Brand Licorice

The reverse side of the card explaining the rules of the competition.

In 1929 the company issued a set of 24 cards featuring contemporary makes of motor cars, each card measuring 2½in (6.4cm) x 1⅝in (4.2cm)

The reason they chose just 24 cards was simple: the name, *Giant Brand Licorice Sweets* consisted of 24 letters, and the name of each motor car depicted started with one of the letters found in that name. So, the first letter 'G' was given to card No 1, the Graham Paige. No 2 – 'I' was an 'Itala' Roadster, No 3 – 'A' was an 'Amilcar' Sedan, and so on.

When we get to Card Number 8, an Austin Saloon was depicted, and simply described as 'Austin Saloon' However it is clear that the model in question is a 16/6, as the 'Austin Six' badge can just make out the on the radiator core, and it also had wire wheels, with which the 16/6s were fitted as standard. The coachwork on this particular vehicle is clearly by a 'local' builder, as a high import duty had been levied on complete motor cars from the UK following the 1914-18 war, so Austin exported just the chassis, and local coachbuilders such as Holden, also based in Melbourne, built their own version of the Austin Burnham Saloon coachwork onto them.

The cars included were:

1. Graham Paige
2. Itala Roadster
3. Amilcar Sedan
4. Nash 400 Sedan
5. Talbot
6. Buick
7. Reo Flying Cloud
8. Austin Saloon
9. Nash 400 Sedan (again)
10. Dodge Sedan
11. Lancia Lambda
12. Itala Tourer
13. Cadillac
14. Oakland Landaulet Sedan
15. Rolls Royce
16. Itala Saloon
17. Chevrolet Sedan
18. Essex Saloon
19. Sunbeam Saloon
20. Whippet
21. Erskin Cabriolet
22. Erskin Saloon
23. Triumph Coupé
24. Standard Saloon

As a point of interest, American makes of car have an American title such as 'Sedan' whereas British makes are referred to as 'Saloons' (where appropriate). Also, for some unknown reason, cards number four and nine feature the same image of the Nash 400 Sedan. There were other versions of the Nash 400, but they chose to use the same image twice. From memory, there was only one other car manufacturer whose name started with 'N' and that was Napier, but they ceased manufacturing motor cars a couple of years before 1929, so there was probably little point including them.

Chapter 4

Zita Austin's nanny

Elizabeth Etherington was just 18 years of age when she went along to the domestic employment bureau in Kidderminster, in the hope that they may have a vacancy for a nanny as she was out of work since her previous employer had sold up and moved abroad.

As it happened, Elizabeth was in luck; the bureau had someone who was looking for a nanny to look after their eleven year old daughter, Zita. Elizabeth arrived at a very large house owned by the Austin Family at Lickey in Worcestershire, and was welcomed by a very smartly dressed lady who told her that she was Mrs Austin and informed her of her duties.

Following a short interview concerning her previous employer and the reasons for her leaving, Elizabeth volunteered the fact that her mother had been a midwife in the nearby village of Hartleberry, which must have made quite a favourable impression on Mrs Austin, because she said "Very well, we look forward to seeing you at Lickey Grange next week."

Lickey Grange, she recalls, was a very large house, in fact it was probably the largest house she had ever seen, and her charge, Miss Zita, was the youngest of the Austin family's three children.

Lickey Grange had a staff of ten, comprised of a cook, kitchen maid, parlour maid, house maid, three gardeners, a chauffeur, a governess and herself, the nanny, who all lived-in at the Grange (with the exception of the governess).

Elizabeth found that Mrs Austin was very easy to get along with – a true lady in every respect – and that she was very kind to her staff. She would always be on hand if ever any of them required help or advice, and would do whatever she could to make their lives as easy for them as possible.

Zita was considered to be quite a frail child and, as such, was not sent to school, but was educated at home. With her being eleven, and Elizabeth just seven years her senior, they got along well, and soon became very good friends. Zita, however, had a mischievous sense of fun, and was always getting up to mischief with her pranks – which were usually at the expense of the other members of the staff.

On one such occasion, as it was beginning to get dark, she came into the nursery holding a very large turnip.

"Come on" she said, "We are going to have some fun with cook." She then started to hollow out the turnip and carve a face on it – similar to the way pumpkins are prepared for Halloween. When she had finished, it looked like a very weird head and she impaled it upon the end of a long stick and then placed a candle inside it.

They both then crept down the stairs and went into the garden, making their way towards the back of the house where the cook could be seen, sorting out some crockery in a small storeroom. Zita lit the candle and slowly raised the illuminated head so that it would appear at the window of the room where the cook was working. They did not have to wait very long before they heard a loud scream as the cook took fright upon seeing the scary apparition at the window. They both quickly abandoned the turnip and stick, and rushed back into the house and up to the nursery without being spotted.

Part of Elizabeth's duties included sleeping in the night nursery with Zita, to wake her up in the morning at seven o'clock, and get her bathed and dressed in readiness for her to join the family for breakfast. However, before she woke her up she would go down to the schoolroom and tidy it up in preparation for her lessons, then, after the morning session they would both go for a walk in the garden until it was time for lunch, which was served at one o'clock, and at which Mr Austin would also be present.

Elizabeth was aware that Mr Austin made motor cars, but she had no idea just how important his company was, or that it was 'world famous' as he rarely, if ever, talked about motor cars when he was at home.

As 'staff,' Elizabeth always took her meals in the servant's dining room. Mrs Austin always made sure that there was plenty of food for them to eat, in fact, she noted that the staff ate almost as well as the family. However, on the occasions when the family were away, leaving Zita in Elizabeth's charge, she would have her meals with her in the dining room, and be waited upon by other members of the staff.

On one occasion, when Mr Austin was about to entertain a very important foreign gentleman, the parlour maid, who usually served at the table, reported in sick, and was unable to do so. Mrs Austin approached Elizabeth to ask her if she would take on that duty for this important dinner, of course she agreed and, although very nervous at the prospect, donned the cap and apron to look the part, even though she had never undertaken such a task before.

The foreign gentleman, as it turned out, spoke very little English and Elizabeth had considerable difficulty in trying to understand what he was saying to her. However, Mrs Austin soon became aware of this, and having caught her eye, was able to signal to her just what it was that he wanted.

Each year during the summer months the Austin family went away for a holiday, which often lasted for a couple of months. During the time Elizabeth was in service with them, they went twice to Torquay in South Devon, and once to the Isle of Wight. Mr Austin would always rent a large, furnished house for their stay, and send two of his staff – which always included Elizabeth – on ahead to prepare it for their arrival.

On their return to Lickey Grange, the smell of autumn was in the air and the family then became focused on the approaching Christmas, which was always a very exciting time for family and staff alike. There was a very large, decorated tree set up in the hall, plenty to eat and drink, and each member of staff received a small present from Mrs Austin. However, in 1914, the commencement of the war was to change all that, and Elizabeth, believing that she should do something to help, reluctantly decided to end her employment with the Austins and become involved in war work.

During the early part of the war she met, fell in love with, and married a guardsman, but that was to end (as many did) with him being killed in action just seven months into their marriage. It was not until 1940 that she married again, this time to someone who had just escaped back to England from France.

A photograph of the imposing frontage of Lickey Grange taken in the late 1990s. (Courtesy J & S Waggett)

Chapter 5

The mystery of two garages

The first two photographs on the next page look very similar to each other. In fact, they are exactly the same shot featuring the same garage. However, the first one depicts a line up of Edwardian Austin motor cars parked outside Prideaux's Hire Depot. They appear to be two 18/24 Endcliffe Phaetons and a 40hp Landaulette – all dating from around 1910-1912, which, of course, is when (and where) the photograph must have been taken.

Whilst it is not easy to make out the full registration numbers of the cars from the photographs, those which can be seen would clearly indicate that they are Devonshire numbers.

Prideaux's, which, at that time, was the sole Austin agent for North Devon, is still around today and is currently located in Barnstable (though this image was taken at its hire depot at Lynton).

The second photograph shows exactly the same line-up of vehicles in front of the exact same garage, but here the name has been changed to 'Duston Garage,' which, as can be seen on the garage sign, is located in Northamptonshire, some 217 miles away.

Now the reasoning behind this is unclear, and we shall probably never know why this subterfuge was carried out, but surely those who went along to the real Duston Garage would have been aware that the premises were nothing like those in the photograph.

Whilst both establishments still remain in business, there was no one at either of them who could provide an answer!

Prideaux Garage circa 1912. Reproduced by kind permission of John Travis, author of *Lynton & Lynmouth: Glimpses of the Past*.

Exactly the same photograph – now shown as Duston Garage, Northampton. (Author's collection)

A 1911 15 horsepower 2-seater coupé which was supplied by Prideaux's Garage of Barnstable to Dr J Harper, the Mayor of Barnstable, who, it was reported, was "very pleased with it." (Courtesy *Austin Advocate* magazine)

Chapter 6

The Austin Sevens that ran on rails

Over the years, Herbert Austin's little Seven has proved itself to be a most versatile motor car, which, when no longer fit to be driven on the road, would probably end up as a small tractor, a lawn mower, or having its sturdy little engine removed and installed in boats to give further service for many a year to come.

However, these conversions were not only confined to aged and time-expired motor cars as, down in Kent, the owners of a nine-inch gauge miniature railway decided that such a car would make an ideal addition to their collection.

The Torry Hill Railway was built in the extensive grounds of York Court, near Sittingbourne, between 1929 and 1930, and runs for 2 miles and 181 yards through woodland, over five arch viaducts, and through a lengthy brick tunnel. It also boasts a long passing loop which permits double train running.

The Austin Seven chosen was a new, 1930 open tourer, which was specially adapted to run on the railway by the Connaught Motor and Carriage Company of Berkeley Street, London, using the car's chassis side members, engine, and gearbox with a modified transmission. It was fitted with two seats in tandem, six flanged wheels and a single headlamp.

A contemporary report in the *Light Car Magazine* of April 1931 reported that "the machine is said to be extremely stable and should prove to be very fast." Unfortunately the opposite proved to be the case, as it was quite unstable and kept falling off the track, and, as a result, it was soon abandoned, left to languish at the back of the workshop until it was eventually broken up several years later with only the wheels remaining.

The converted Austin Seven, designed to run on the 9in gauge Torry Hill Railway. (Courtesy *Light Car Magazine*)

The Torry Hill Railway is still operational with steam-powered locomotives, which are all based on actual rolling stock from the 1930s, and include scaled down examples of an Atlantic, a Nelson, and a King class built in the 1950s and 1960s, but regrettably without an Austin Seven to run with them.

However, a rather more successful attempt at running an Austin Seven on rails can be attributed to the South African Railways, who, in 1930 had 16 Austin Seven two-seater touring cars converted in their Johannesburg workshops to run on rails, in order to enable 'permanent way' staff to inspect the tracks.

The 9in gauge railway at Torry Hill, near Sittingbourne, Kent. (Author's collection)

The locomotive behind the Austin in the photograph was considered to be the largest and fastest in use on South African lines at that time, but, according to the *Cape Times*, the little Austin Seven was able to climb gradients at 25mph and achieve 60mph on the level, and, in a test over a timed distance on the Pretoria-Irene Line, it beat the express locomotive by just over a minute – but then, I suppose it would have needed to do that with such a vast mass of steaming iron and steel running so close behind it!

One of the 16 Austin Seven tourers, modified within the Johannesburg railway workshops to run on the South African Railway. (Courtesy *Cape Times*)

Chapter 7

Driving Miss Daisy

In 1973 my wife and I decided to spend a holiday on the Isle of Wight, and that we would drive there in our fabric-bodied 1929 Austin 16/6 saloon car. One reason being that in the quarterly magazine published by the Automobile Association (AA) around that time there was an article written about an eighty-year-old lady living in Bembridge who was still driving the 1928 Austin 16/6 that her father had purchased for her in 1930, which also had a fabric body, identical to ours.

Daisy when interviewed for the *AA Magazine* at Bembridge. (Courtesy Automobile Association)

That lady was Daisy Fearon, who had spent most of her young life in India and China where her father worked in the Diplomatic Service. She learned to drive during the First World War, transporting everything from coal to wounded soldiers.

On their return from overseas in 1930, the Fearon family moved to Caterham in Surrey, which was where the Austin was purchased through the Austin Dealership. Her father had been advised that the latest (1930) models were not a patch on the earlier ones, and that if he was prepared to wait, the dealer knew of a very good 1928 16/6 which was due to be part exchanged within just next few weeks. When the car was purchased, Daisy named it 'PK' from the Registration Number PK 1462.

In the interview for the *AA Magazine,* she confided to the editor, David Owen, that she could not drive modern cars as the steering wheel was "right there in your lap," they have no room inside and they did not provide a proper view. During the early years of her ownership she used the car extensively to travel long distances abroad – mainly to France and Italy.

Our meeting with Daisy Fearon went well and, as you can see from the photograph on the next page, the two identical Austins stood happily side by side in her driveway with Andrew, our fourteen-month-old son, hanging onto the front bumper.

The following story is told by Martin Woodward, who was always on hand to get Daisy out of the many situations she managed to get herself into whilst she was out driving her car when she was well into her seventies.

The author at Daisy's house with the two identical Austin 16/6s.

Daisy Fearon lived in a tumble down house across the road from where I lived as a child in Bembridge, on the Isle of Wight. She was always considered to be one of those 'village characters' that every small community possesses, and she used to fascinate me with tales of her family life in China and other colonial locations that her family were posted to.

Daisy never married and was frequently seen driving her Austin around the island roads. When I was a child it was common to hear the cry: "Watch out! Here comes Miss Fearon," and we would all dive for cover, as her driving was a bit unpredictable at times. It was always a guess as to which side of the road she would actually be driving on during any particular day. She nearly always wore a wide brimmed hat, from under which she would peer out through the windscreen, adding to her already slightly eccentric image.

There were several amusing incidents over the years, but I will only quote a couple of the more memorable ones.

Back in the 1960s, Daisy was driving to Newport one day, a distance of about 12 miles, and there was a crossroads on the way at Brading. At this point, the main road from Ryde crossed the route that Daisy was taking, and she was supposed to stop and give way at the junction. For some reason she failed to do this and carried straight on, colliding with a large Luton box van in the process. The Luton van was impaled on the front of the Austin, and was a total write-off, but Daisy calmly reversed out of the wreckage, drove around it and continued on her trip to Newport. Naturally she was later apprehended for this slight oversight and there was a subsequent court case during which she was asked why she failed to stop after the accident. Her reply was: "Well, the engines were still going, so I thought everything was alright, and I did have some shopping to do!" Daisy always referred to 'the engines' of the car, and I often wondered whether she actually thought there were two of them under the bonnet. The Austin, needless to say, survived the incident virtually unscathed (apart from a few bruises).

The next incident was particularly memorable for me, and occurred a few years later, in 1971. Daisy used to have quite a few knocks with the Austin, mainly whilst getting in and out of her small garage, and I think I rebuilt the nearside wing for her about seven times in all. All the work I did on the car was done on a favour basis, as I had known Daisy for so long, and I was very keen on old vehicles myself, having had several old cars in the past. As a result, she would usually ring me if she had trouble with the Austin.

On this particular occasion, she phoned to say that the 'engines' would not restart after she had been visiting a friend's house, so, I told her to wait where she was until I got there. At that time I had a Ford Escort van which I only used for work, so I took that as it had a tow bar on the back. On arrival, I spent a fair while explaining to Daisy the wonders of a towed 'bump-start.' She looked totally bemused by this, and the first attempt saw me towing her along, with her on the wrong side of the road and the rope at an angle between us. With nothing else happening, I stopped the van and again explained that she had to switch on the ignition, disengage then engage the clutch, etc, and when the engine fired, I would put my hand out of the van window, give a slow-down signal, then pull into the side of the road to remove the rope.

Well, we set off again, with local residents diving for cover as I towed her, erratically, up the road. Suddenly, I heard the loud revving of the Austin's 'engines' behind me, dutifully gave the 'slowing down' hand signal, and pulled in to the side of the road. The next thing I knew, I was being pulled 180 degrees around in the road, as Daisy overtook me and sped off homeward, trailing the broken tow rope behind her. Fortunately for me (and the van), I had used a relatively weak tow rope which snapped, otherwise I would have been towed to her house backwards. As it was, I was left turned in the opposite direction with the van facing the driver behind, who had witnessed the whole event. He was laughing hysterically in the middle of the road, and said that it was the funniest thing he had ever seen.

When I eventually stopped laughing sufficiently to be able to drive the van again. I turned it around and drove to Daisy's house, to find her in the kitchen putting on the kettle for tea.

"Why ... " I asked incredulously, " ... didn't you wait until I had untied the tow rope?"

"Well." She replied. "The engines had fired up, so I thought I had better get on home." What could I say? I just laughed. Without characters like her in life, we would have no good stories to tell.

Daisy died in 1974 at the age of 84, still driving the Austin virtually to the end. She had owned PK for a total of 44 years.

Naturally, Daisy was well known on the Isle of Wight, and was fondly observed, mostly from a safe distance, by the locals. It has to be said that she was a law unto herself: she parked the Austin wherever she wanted, never recognising yellow lines – single or double – and woe betide any traffic warden who dared to tell her otherwise.

The author's wife, son Andrew, and Daisy – plus, of course, the two Austin 16/6s.

Chapter 8

Singing about the Austin Seven

Over the years there have been several songs written and sung about certain makes of motor car, such as the Oldsmobile with *My Merry Oldsmobile*, the Stanley Steamer, the Cadillac, the Model A Ford with *Henry's Made a Lady Out of Lizzy*, and the *The Rhythm of the Road*, which was about the new Ford V-8. and then of course there was the *Austin Unity Song*, which I covered in my previous book. All of the above, with perhaps the exception of the *Unity Song*, were designed to promote the virtues of the make or model of the car about which they were composed, but *My Little Austin Seven* was written purely for entertainment, and was not endorsed in any way by the Austin Motor Company – though it is believed that, secretly, they quite approved of it!

From the moment the Austin Seven was launched, it was to be held up to ridicule in many different ways. In chapter 11 you will see a number of examples in which it was made fun of, but here we will take a look at a couple of Austin Seven songs which were released during the latter part of the 1920s.

The first one, entitled *Oh, I Would Like A Baby Austin* – which was not very well known, was released on the Piccadilly label, and sung by Jim Kelleher who was accompanied by the Piccadilly Hotel Dance Band.

The Piccadilly label for *I Would Like A Baby Austin.*

Lyrics for *Oh, I would like a Baby Austin*:

Oh I would like a baby Austin.
One between us two.
Wouldn't it be fun,
Just a little one, take it out together when our work is done.
Just a baby Austin,
Then I'd be ever true.
Oh I would like a baby Austin,
Just a dear little car for two.

Whilst this particular song was rather short on lyrics, yes, that was the full complement of lyrics, it has to be said that the accompaniment was very catchy.

The second song was, of course *My Little Austin Seven* with lyrics by Clarkson Rose and set to music by Norman Long.

Entertainer and composer Norman Long.

Entertainer and composer Clarkson Rose.

Both Clarkson Rose and Norman Long recorded this song, each presenting it in their own particular style.

Norman Long was an English entertainer, born in 1893 in the South London town of Sydenham. After the First World War he embarked upon a career as an insurance salesman, but also found the time to write music which gently mocked the establishment. When being introduced as an entertainer it was as 'Norman Long: A Song, a Smile, and a Piano,' but later, when he began broadcasting on the radio, it was changed to 'A Song, a Joke and a Piano' when the 'smile' became irrelevant. Norman Long died in 1951, aged 58.

Clarkson Rose was also an English entertainer and song writer, and is probably best known for his comic song about owning an Austin Seven. Born Arthur C Rose in Dudley, Worcestershire in 1890, Clarkson Rose began his working life as a bank clerk, entertaining in his spare time. Whilst still in his teens, he formed an eight-strong concert party and began dabbling in serious theatre. He was also one of Britain's best-loved music hall and variety comedians, and a celebrated pantomime dame whose slightly naughty touring review *Twinkle* was a star attraction at British holiday resorts for many years.

Clarkson Rose was also a prolific recording artist and, between 1922 and 1937, he and his wife, Olive, produced over 150 songs for HMV's economy label, Zonophone. *My Little Austin Seven* made its appearance on 25th January, 1929. Rose probably had no real affinity for Herbert's 'baby,' but, with the depression in the wind, the timing of this cheeky little send up – adapted for Columbia by Rose's close contemporary, Norman Long – was exquisite, and should have been received at Longbridge with gratitude. But was it ..? I wonder. Clarkson Rose died in the April of 1968, aged 77.

In the early 1970s, permission was granted to reproduce *My Little Austin Seven* by Clarkson Rose onto a 7in Vinyl record, together with *The Austin Unity Song*. When the stock of these ran out, both songs were digitally re-mastered and re-issued as a CD.

The Columbia record label for *My Little Austin Seven*.

Lyrics for *My Little Austin Seven*:

Nearly everybody's got a motor car today
Whatever make it is, it's quite the best of all, they say.
You can have your Morris Cowleys and your Essex Six,
Believe me, they're not in it with my little box of tricks.

It's an Austin Seven, a little baby Austin,
The cutest little car upon the road.
I can drive it anywhere, you ought to see it clamber,
Upstairs, downstairs, in my lady's chamber.
It matters not at all if it is a trifle small,
Believe me boy it's heaven.
If you want to give the wife a ride without all her relations
You cannot beat an Austin Seven.

It's an Austin Seven a little baby Austin,
The cutest little car upon the road.
I can drive it anywhere, you ought to see it clamber,
Upstairs, downstairs, in the lady's chamber.
It matters not at all, if you think it's rather small,
It never stops, but if it does you only need a shove
To drive a little Austin Seven.

The house I live in hasn't got a garage and what's more
I don't intend to build one it's a waste of time, I'm sure
'Cause we've got a lovely cubby hole behind the kitchen door
That'll hold my little Austin Seven.

The other day I went out driving in a shower of rain
And that's a thing, believe me, I shall never do again
For we skidded in the gutter and we got washed down a drain
In my tricky little Austin Seven.

One day I met an omnibus that stretched from side to side
Across the road and held up all the traffic far and wide
I just drove underneath it and came out the other side
In my dainty little Austin Seven.

Once I saw an Advert for a secretary so,
I drove up to the office and the manager said "Oh"
Have you a portable typewriter ?
I said "no, it's my little Austin Seven."

Once a motorcyclist drove up and staggered me,
"Thank God!" he said, "I've found you, alright now ..." said he
And in place of where his sidecar used to be
He fastened on my Austin Seven.

When driving in the park, a nurse struck up a parlay and
She said, "Now don't you move, I am surprised at you I am"
She thought I was the baby she'd left sitting in the pram
In my little Austin Seven.

It's an Austin Seven, a little baby Austin,
The cutest little car upon the road.
I can drive it anywhere, you ought to see it clamber
Upstairs, downstairs, in my lady's chamber.

I've got a Ma-in-Law, and you know just how they jaw
And she's fourteen stone eleven,

**But she has to keep her knees up and it stops her chin from wagging
In the back seat of my Austin Seven.**

**If I ever want to park it and the police ask what I'm at,
I never have to worry about a little thing like that,
I just bung it in the cloakroom with my overcoat and hat,
My little Austin Seven.**

**An early Austin Chummy exported to New Zealand.
(Courtesy of *The New Zealand Vintage Austin Register*)**

Front cover of sheet music for *My Little Austin Seven*.

Chapter 9

Alf Depper – an Austin pioneer

The name 'Alf Depper' is probably not one that readily springs to mind when reviewing the history of the Austin Motor Company, but thanks to a recorded interview, which Barry Quann (the then editor of the Austin house magazine, *BMC World*) conducted with him on 4th April 1967, we can paint a very comprehensive picture of the various parts Alf played in his years working at The Austin.

Alf Depper's father was employed as the resident engineer at the Rubery Hill Hospital, and it was here that young Alf first became interested in engineering. Whenever he could, he would accompany his father and assist him with some of the tasks he had to manage. This, of course, did not go unnoticed by his father, who decided that, when Alf left the Rubery Board School at the age of 14, he should be seeking an apprenticeship to learn the trade properly.

In order to pursue this further, Alf's father wrote to Herbert Austin at his newly established motor car factory to tell him that his son was a bright lad who might make a career in the business, and that he would benefit from serving an apprenticeship with Austin. Herbert Austin wrote back saying that the Austin Motor Company was not currently taking on apprentices, but that was something which it was seriously contemplating, however he would very much like to meet this bright lad and, if suited, offer him a job.

STARTING WORK

After a short interview conducted by Herbert Austin, Alf was offered a job as a shop boy in the marking off section at a weekly wage of five shillings (25p). He started work there on 28th February 1906, just a few weeks after the factory opened.

One of the first jobs he was given was to 'mark off' No. 1 gearbox for the very first Austin from the drawings under the guidance and watchful eye of Herbert Austin's younger brother, Harry. At the end of the week, Alf received his first pay packet which was handed to him in a small tin box, about two inches in diameter and an inch thick. In the top was a small 'D' shaped hole through which the coins were placed. On returning home he gave the money over to his mother.

Alf remained in the marking off section for about eight months, after which he moved into the fitting shop where he was involved in lining brake shoes. Following that, he moved on to the gearbox section, then back axles, then the engine section and on to services, by which time the 1914-18 war was just about to start.

SENT TO RUSSIA

By this time, Alf was just into his 22nd year, and he was asked to sail to Archangel to meet up with a consignment of armoured cars and 2/3-ton lorries which were due to be delivered, having been purchased by the Imperial Russian Army for the newly-formed Russian Army Automobile Corps. This order came as a direct result of successful field trials of the 40hp Austin Defiant in 1908/09, following the evaluation of a number of vehicles from numerous manufacturers for reliability and suitability for use in the field.

The order for these vehicles came at a good time for the Austin Motor Company, as there was little work on the books, and some of the factory was practically closed. The Russian Commission came over to the factory and simply placed an order for everything that was available with the 20hp chassis – which were to be built as ambulances back in Russia, the 30hp – to be built as armoured cars, and the 2/3-ton lorries – made into spares lorries, heavy ambulances and workshops complete with small lathes.

Alf landed at Archangel in October 1914. His was the last boat to get through because the ice-breakers could no longer keep the harbour open. He spent the next two to three weeks there preparing to travel overland to St Petersburg (which, at that time, was called Petrograd) to meet up with the vehicles which had all come via Vladivostok. There, he was needed to retune them to run on poor quality Russian petrol.

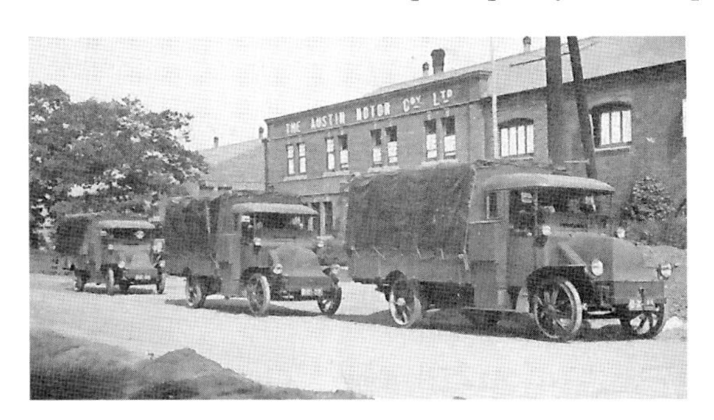

Three of the 2/3-ton lorries destined for Russia. (Courtesy *Austin Advocate* magazine)

The Russians were impressed with the Austin, as the only other vehicles available at that time were Crossleys and Rudge Whitworth motorcycles, which were good for their specific purpose, but Austin vehicles proved more useful.

The Russian soldiers, Alf noted, were a rather rough lot, and he was given the responsibility for training half a dozen of them to drive and maintain the vehicles. Their lack of enthusiasm was marked by the need to watch over them all the time to ensure that when asked to tighten a nut, they actually did it – he ended up doing most of the work himself as they were clearly not that interested.

Due to the sub-zero temperatures and, of course, the absence of antifreeze, all the radiators had to be drained every day when the vehicles were idle. The temperatures were so cold that if any bare skin touched any metal it would burn and leave the flesh stuck behind. However, in spite of all this, the Austin vehicles provided excellent service and were much respected.

Alf's stay in Russia was brought to an end by the onset of The Russian Revolution, and he and the other mechanics were advised to leave as soon as possible. Their return journey was via Finnish-Karonge, Swedish-Karonge, Stockholm and then back to England.

WORKING ON AIRCRAFT

On his return from Russia Alf was assigned to work on the development of fighter aircraft for the Ministry of War. He recalled working for a Swiss designer by the name of Haefeli who had designed a 250hp twelve-cylinder aircraft engine, the bearings of which were all roller, with not a single plain white metal bearing in the entire engine. Six of the conrods, which looked something like frying pans, were fed in from one end, and six fed in from the other. Aircraft design was still very much in its infancy, and designers and manufacturers were constantly looking to achieve the optimum power from what was currently available. This particular twelve-cylinder engine, therefore, underwent a number of modifications to both lighten it and increase its power output. Ultimately, it was modified to have most of the cast iron replaced with aluminium and it finally turned out to be a very good and powerful engine.

Another significant feature of the Hafeli engine was a gun tube that was designed to provide the strength of the engine, the crankcase being made in two halves and bolted around the tube in order for the shell to be fired through the centre of the propeller, instead of having to provide an interrupter to allow the shell to fire through the arc of the propeller blades.

Alf's time in the aircraft section nearly came to an untimely end when, on starting up an aircraft engine by swinging the propeller, it came back rather too quickly and hit him. Fortunately, the engine had just started up and did no appreciable damage.

By the time the war ended Alf had been promoted to chargehand at the very young age of 26.

After the war, the Austin Motor Company endeavoured to get back to catering to the private motorist, who, it considered, would include many ex-servicemen who had learnt new driving skills and would be looking for motor vehicles – and indeed even light aircraft – to purchase.

However, the decision to concentrate on the 'Twenty Horse' (the twenty horsepower Austin or Austin Twenty), together with high taxation on such vehicles did the Austin Motor Company no favours, and it was very soon struggling financially which lead it to being placed into the hands of a receiver. The design of the Austin Whippet aircraft, whilst advanced for its time did not find favour either, as there was a glut of ex-RFC/RAF fighter planes at a price considerably less than that of a new Austin Whippet, as a consequence, only five of them were ever built.

THE AUSTIN TWENTY

The Austin Twenty was, however, a very well designed motor car, and capable of a reasonably good speed (if correctly tuned and driven in the right hands). In the interview with *BMC World*, Alf recalls the Twenty Sports which Captain Waite and the chargehand tester, Lew Kings, drove at Shelsey Walsh. It was later entered at Brooklands where it won its first race on a handicap. Captain Waite was, of course, Lord Austin's son-in-Law, and a former captain in the Australian Army. As well as being involved in the racing side of the Company, he held the official position of managing the finished test and car despatch department. It was during a race with Captain Waite that Alf's life nearly came to an untimely end, when he was acting as mechanic during the Irish TT, at a place called Ballystockart. It had been raining very heavily, and the car was going very well and heading for victory, when all of a sudden the car went off the road, hit the edge, came back, and both Alf and Captain Waite were thrown from the vehicle. Alf was knocked out for about six hours and he carried the scars from the blackthorn hedge in which he landed for the rest of his life.

THE AUSTIN SEVEN

When the 'Seven Horse Project' started, Alf was put in charge of building the first half dozen. The idea of a Seven horsepower car started up at Lickey Grange, where Austin had brought in a young lad called Stanley Edge from the Works Drawing Office to assist in laying out the drawings. Austin then brought in a chap called Stott, who was a body designer; both worked under the governor's instructions in great secrecy, because at that time, the project had to be kept separate from the factory as it was now being run by the receivers.

When the drawings were completed Austin moved the project down to the Works where it then became a factory project. It was about this time when Alf received a reprimand from Mr Austin. A bolt that was to be fitted into the frame (chassis) was marked-out to go into a round hole, but Alf had decided that this should be hexagonal in order to secure it against turning. When Austin saw this unauthorised modification he blew his top, accusing him of scrapping a perfectly good frame. Alf stood his ground and argued his case, and as a consequence all further frames were modified with a hexagonal hole.

Alf was involved in the machining of all the first Austin Seven engine castings, and for building up the engine. The complete car was to be finished and ready for the road before Easter 1922, it was, however, actually finished during the evening of Easter Saturday. At 6:30pm Austin invited Alf to accompany him on its very first journey, which was to take them out through the factory gates and up the Lickey Road. The little car performed very well indeed, and they soon found themselves heading, not surprisingly, towards Lickey Grange. When they arrived, Lady Austin came out to greet them and, of course, to see the car that her husband had been spending all his time on.

"Well, what do you think about this?" said Austin. Lady Austin looked it over and commented that it needed cleaning. "Then come and clean it," replied her husband.

After checking it over, they drove off down Wychbold where the wireless station used to be, and then back to the Works. Its first long run covered successfully without any problems.

Production started directly after that first test run. It was slow progress as each one was hand built for at least a couple of months until such time as all the jigs and fixtures, which also had to be made by hand, could be put in place.

RACING THE SEVEN

The Austin Seven was launched through the newspapers in mid 1922, and the first the public came to see of it was at the Motor Show in Olympia, West London. The following year it was entered, and won its first race at Brooklands.

It took Alf and Captain Waite about four days to drive down to Brooklands from the factory. They reached the other side of Reddich only to discover that the little car was not geared highly enough, so they returned to the Works to put in a higher gear. They then set off again to Weybridge only to run a big end bearing on the way, at Sunrising. With that repaired they set off again when, just before reaching Banbury, something went 'BANG!' Upon being towed to a garage at Banbury, it was discovered that the camshaft gear had broken in two. This was on the Easter Sunday. They telephoned the 'Guvnor,' who happened to be up at the Works and, as components were now coming through production, it was arranged for one of the team to return to the Works and collect the replacement gear. Alf stripped down the engine using the garage's tools and workshop facilities and, when the new part arrived from the Works, replaced the damaged one with it. The work was completed by 7pm that evening.

They decided to stay overnight at Banbury, and then make an early start the next morning for Brooklands, with Captain Waite driving the Seven at a steady pace.

When, at 11am, they eventually arrived at Brooklands, the track was closed. The team was denied the facility of driving around the track – as would have been expected – so, in order to fill in the time, they busied themselves carrying out a few minor jobs on the car (including altering the carburettor jets, which Alf thought could provide a richer mixture).

The bell telling competitors to assemble at the starting line sounded and Captain Waite made his way over to the Vickers Sheds. The bell sounded a second time to start and the race and away went Captain Waite. Round and round he went and came first in the first race, establishing the Austin Seven as a true winner, putting it firmly on the path of success.

EARLY RACING DAYS

Alf was not unfamiliar with Brooklands because, as a lad of just 16, he was asked to go down to the track with the 1908 racing Austins to work on them. A fortnight after winning a race there, the Company received an invitation to attend the opening of the track at Monza where, again, the Austin was lucky enough to win the Grand Prix of Italy for the Company.

Racing was to play a major part in Alf Depper's life, for that was the area of work in which he was to spend his entire career whilst in the production development section of the Company.

Racing, it had to be said, was something in which Herbert Austin took a very keen interest; it was his belief that by taking a normal production vehicle, and pitting it against the best offered by other manufacturers, you would ultimately end up with a better designed product for your customers.

By 1924 Alf had set up a 'racing stable' for the Company where the Seven could be prepared for events held at venues such as Brooklands, Shelsey Walsh, The Boulogne Grand Prix, and Le Mans (before it became a 24-hour race). All the Sevens used in these races were basic production models, manufactured to exactly the same specification as those sent to the distributors. However, once they reached the experimental department's workshop, the engine underwent some basic changes, such as replacing the camshaft and fine-tuning the engine.

It was just before the outbreak of the Second World War that Alf was promoted to become the chief experimental engineer within the production development division – in his own modest way Alf admits in the interview that there was only him on the job, which was agreed to between the shop and the drawing office.

Alf Depper seated in an early Austin Seven circa 1932. (Courtesy Bob Wyatt)

ANOTHER WAR AND ON TO THE MINI

The war put paid to any further ideas of racing, and all efforts were directed towards providing munitions to satisfy the insatiable appetite of the war machine. Alf remembers his work in the development of aero engines and a tank engine called the Meteorite in about 1941.

Once the war was over, research and development focused once again on private cars, and the first new model to be put into production was the A40 'Devon' saloon. Alf worked on the development of these and the first two experimental 'Atlantics.'

In Alf's final years at The Austin, he worked on prototypes for the 1100 and 1800 projects and, of course, the Mini, which he liked very much. The first experimental Mini took to the road looking very much like the A35 to disguise it from industrial spies.

Alf finally retired from work in 1966 when he was just 65, after devoting 50 years of his life to the Company When Alf's father noticed that his son had a keen interest and ability where engineering was concerned he was certainly not far off the mark, and that letter that he sent to Mr Herbert Austin requesting an interview for a 'bright lad' certainly paid off handsomely.

Earl Howe sharing a joke with Arthur Waite and Alf Depper at the 1930 Double Twelve Event. (Courtesy Bob Wyatt)

Lord Austin's eldest daughter, Irene Waite, presenting a gift to Alf Depper on the occasion of the Golden Jubilee of the Austin Motor Company. The inscription reads: "With many thanks for all you did for Daddie and Colonel Waite over many years. Yours sincerely. Irene Waite. 1955." (Courtesy Bob Wyatt)

Alf Depper looking somewhat reflectively at a 1932 Box Saloon Seven. (Courtesy Bob Wyatt)

Chapter 10

Maple Leaf IV

In 1912, the Austin Motor Company had begun looking into the production of marine engines for small sailing craft. At that time there was strong competition, especially between the United Kingdom, France, and The United States of America, in seeing just how fast the craft could go over water.

The British International trophy, or The Harmsworth Trophy as it was better known, was held annually in the home waters of the previous year's winner. In 1912, Maple leaf IV, piloted by Thomas Sopwith Snr at New York's Huntington Bay, won the trophy for Great Britain with a speed of 43.18 knots, so the 1913 event was held in Britain, at Osborne Bay off the Isle of Wight, as part of the Cowes Regatta.

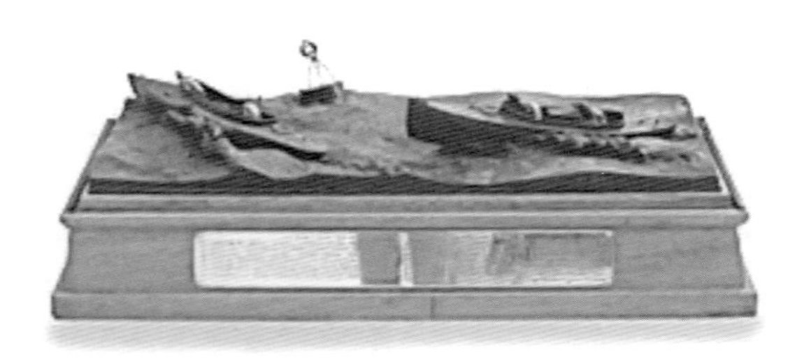

The coveted Harmsworth Trophy.

Maple Leaf IV was owned by Sir Edward Mackay Edgar, a wealthy, Canadian-born banker, who took a very keen interest in this sport, and already had three boats specially built for such competitions.

This, his latest boat, was a five-step Saunders-Fauber Hydroplane, designed and built by S E Saunders at its yard in Cowes on the Isle of Wight.

Adjusting the massive engines. (Courtesy *Austin Advocate* magazine)

However, the powerful 350hp V12 engines installed in Maple Leaf IV, were found to be too heavy to provide the speed required to win this trophy, so the Austin Motor Company were called in to offer advice, and undertake any alterations which they considered may be necessary.

Austin engineers working on Maple Leaf's 350hp V12 engines. (Courtesy *Austin Advocate* magazine)

Their remit was to make both the engines lighter using as many of the original parts as possible. On examination, they found that the cylinders were designed in such a way as to prevent enough space between them to ensure sufficient cooling when under extreme pressure. This would cause the cylinders to run red hot and subsequently crack the pistons.

Austin's design engineers considered that the entire cooling system of the engines needed to be redesigned in order to provide the extra cooling that was required. Other modifications included the lightening of the pistons, which, together with the cylinders were accurately reground after being machined.

Improvements were also carried out on the valve gear – with new valves manufactured from a high nickel content steel. Also in for close inspection was the lubrication, which was fed to each bearing at 20lbs of pressure, with surplus oil draining into the bottom of the crankcase; from there it was pumped into a cooler and then back into the supply tank.

Another problem was that the exhaust pipes were found to be larger than they actually needed to be, and, furthermore, were located in such a position as to make access to the valve gear almost impossible. Here the design engineers were able to completely alter the layout by fitting large diameter water-cooled pipes to each cylinder.

The next area of concern was the arrangement of the induction pipes and carburation: the engines, as originally supplied, were each fitted with one pipe and a huge carburettor, the combined weight of which was excessive, and obviously played a significant part in their overall inefficiency. In the redesigned layout, the induction pipes took the form of two straight, horizontal tubes, one for each set of cylinders. These were joined together at either end with each pipe having a small, separate White

& Poppe carburettor. This revised system ensured that there was always a continuous circulation of gas flowing in one direction, enabling each cylinder to obtain a full charge.

The power was conveyed to the propeller through clutches and reduction gears involving two gearboxes which were designed by Austin. These were manufactured using aluminium castings to help in reducing the overall weight. The gears themselves were manufactured from both steel and bronze, with the shafts running on Hoffman ball bearings. Only one of the boxes was fitted with a reverse gear.

In redesigning the engine, whilst every effort was made in reducing the weight, it was important to ensure that the strength and reliability was never compromised; in fact, the overall weight when finished was slightly more than before they started, however, the redesigned engine proved to be much more powerful with the 7in bore and 7½in piston stroke remaining the same as before. The redesigned engines were now capable of returning 400hp each when under pressure, but were normally being maintained at a modest 380hp.

Out on the Solent, Maple Leaf IV at speed.
(Courtesy *Austin Advocate* magazine)

Further sea trials on the Solent.
(Courtesy *Austin Advocate* magazine)

Bow lifting out of the water, Maple Leaf IV ready and able to win the trophy.

The modifications carried out by The Austin Motor Company proved to be most satisfactory as, again, with Thomas Sopwith Snr. at the controls, Maple Leaf IV secured the trophy for Great Britain whilst attaining a speed of 57,45 knots (66.1mph) and was the first boat to reach 50 knots since the race first began in 1903.

The start of the Great War saw the cancellation of any further attempts, and the trophy was suspended until 1920 when it was again held at Osborne Bay. Maple Leaf IV was not entered in this (or any subsequent) race, and the trophy was now back in the hands of America's Garfield Wood with Miss America I, which had attained a speed of 61.51 knots (70.78 mph).

It is understood that on the commencement of WWI, Sir Edward Mackay Edgar offered Maple Leaf IV to the Admiralty for use as a fast naval patrol boat, but this offer was rejected due to the fact that (according to the Admiralty) it used too much petrol!

Mr Garfield Wood, owner of Miss America I, holding the trophy he had just won for the United States.

Chapter 11

Funny little Austin Sevens

In the entire history of the automobile, there cannot have been a motor car that was so loved and revered, and yet also the subject of so much ridicule as Herbert Austin's little Austin Seven.

When it was first launched at the 1922 Motor Show at Olympia, the motoring press and public were, it has to be said, quite sceptical about Herbert Austin's diminutive motor car. However it not only turned out to be a life saver for the Company but a car which was not only fun to drive, but was as robust and reliable as its big brothers, The 12/4 and the Twenty. What is probably most remarkable is that almost 100 years since it was introduced there are several thousand of them still giving their owners considerable pleasure, just the way that Herbert Austin intended.

It was not long before cartoonists started to make good capital out of the Seven's size, and as we saw in Chapter 8, just seven years after its launch it even had two songs written about it. This chapter takes a look at some of the cartoons that were published in the press in and around the 1920s and also some of the weird and wonderful creations with which it was embellished for fun, advertising, or raising money for charity.

In the strip cartoon opposite which was published in the *Austin Advocate* magazine of July 1927. Magnus Motors, which were major distributors of Austin Motor vehicles in New Zealand, tells of what New Zealand motorists thought of the Seven. Clearly the Austin Motor Company thought this to be good publicity for them too.

The next cartoon was typical of many which appeared during the early years of the car's production. In this 1926 cartoon published in *Punch* magazine the constable is telling the owner of the Austin that his car was causing an obstruction, to which the motorist replied: "What am I obstructing the road or the drain?"

Then, the lady of the house is telling the person outside that she could not come to his aid because she was "washing the baby."

The driver of the limousine is asking his passenger what he thought about the Austin Seven that they were about to overtake. The passenger replied, flicking the ash from his cigarette into the car, that they made "topping ashtrays!"

Our final cartoon shows an Austin Seven driving in the opposite direction to a large two seater sports car. The wife of the Austin owner tells her husband how proud she is that they were able to afford a four-seater motor car.

July, 1927 — The ADVOCATE

What they think of the Austin 'Seven' in New Zealand

(Reproductions of an Austin Agents' Advertisement).

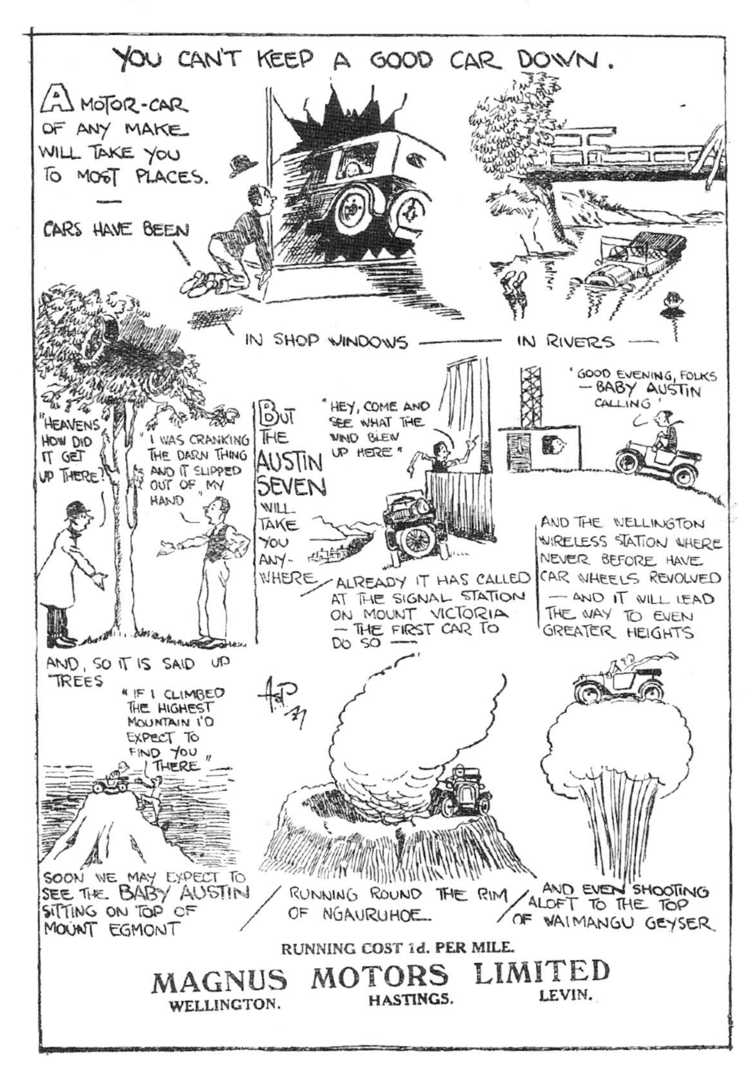

Magnus Motors cartoon. (Courtesy *Austin Advocate* magazine)

CONSTABLE: "THIS WON'T DO, SIR. I MUST HAVE YOUR NAME FOR CAUSING AN OBSTRUCTION."
MOTORIST: "OBSTRUCTION! WHAT AM I OBSTRUCTING—THE ROAD OR THE DRAIN?"

Punch Magazine cartoon.

"I can't come out, I'm washing the baby."

Moving away from cartoons, we now take a look at some of the ingenious ways in which some companies took advantage of the Austin Seven's diminutive size in order to promote products. The following examples show, not only a couple of the ingenious ideas, but the skill of the coachbuilders who were commissioned to change a motor car or van into a mobile advert for their customers.

The first photograph shows an open tourer transformed for Dunlop into a bicycle saddle, whilst the second one was a 'C' cab van converted to promote Morgan Brothers

Using the small open car as an ashtray!

Proud of their little four-seater.

of Swansea which traded in exide batteries. Both of these were from the early to mid 1920s.

Advertising of this kind was not just restricted to the United Kingdom. In the following two photographs (both from *Austin Advocate* magazine), we see how promotion of the Austin Seven was conducted in India.

The top photograph shows an early (1923-4) Chummy mounted on what appears to be an American truck, whilst the second photograph was taken a few years later to promote the launch of a late 1920s tourer which was due to be available from The Indian Motors at Easter.

The Austin Seven was of course converted to represent many things, and not just for commercial products, the final collection of photographs show some of the ingenious ways in which their owners perhaps won prizes participating in carnival parades – or just purely for the fun of it.

The Dunlop Saddle. (Courtesy *Austin Advocate* magazine)

Advertising exide batteries. (Courtesy Bob Wyatt)

One way of advertising an Austin Seven in India!

And another!

The first two play upon the Austin's size and its 'Baby' tag. The top one shows 'Aunty Smiler' as a nanny pushing her two babies in the pram. The second deploys a similar theme but with a normal size nanny.

The 'baby' image was well represented. (Courtesy *Austin Advocate* magazine)

A slightly different angle on the same theme. (Courtesy *Austin Advocate* magazine)

A pretty girl sitting on a crinoline dress atop ... Yes, an Austin Seven! (Courtesy *Austin Advocate* magazine)

attempt to cross the road to meet up with his girlfriend (played by Lesley-Ann Down), bumped quite heavily into the back of the Austin. On the same film I noticed that when changing gear my knuckles were knocking the dashboard, something that clearly should not be happening. It turned out that the base of the gearlever had fractured and was very near the point of coming away in my hand. Fortunately there was a welder working on site who very kindly repaired the fracture quite quickly.

I had always stipulated that I was to be the only person allowed to drive my car, which, of course gave me additional earnings as an extra, but the filming of the London Weekend Television production of *We The Accused* was to take place up in the Lake District, and for the length of time it would be required I was unable to take time off from work. So, on this one occasion, I entrusted my car to a long standing friend and Austin owner who would take the car up on his trailer, and do any driving required. The Austin was to be the police car in which the Detective Inspector (played by Ian Cuthbertson) set out to hunt down two fleeing fugitives.

All went well until the timing chain slipped a couple of teeth causing the engine to misfire quite badly and then overheat. This caused the top hose to burst and also affected the temperature of the petrol which evaporated as it was about to enter the carburettor; then – as if this was not bad enough – the tail pipe fell off and needed to be welded back on again. Then an oil seal gave up on the rear nearside brake drum which saturated the brake linings with grease. The cable brakes of most Austin motor cars were probably not the most efficient, and grease on brake linings did not exactly help matters in this respect, as was discovered by a young female production assistant who narrowly escaped being run over when she stood in front of it, indicating the exact spot where the car was required to stop. Fortunately, she was not too badly hurt.

My friend, although owning an Austin himself, failed to either rectify the faults or contact me to ask for my advice. Had it not been for veteran actor Ian Cuthbertson's insistence that, in spite of the car's problem, the Austin was right for the role as his police car, it would have been sent home and replaced with something else.

When the time came to bring the car back home, a near collision involving the towing vehicle caused the driver to brake suddenly and the Austin, which had not been secured properly, moved forward on the trailer and hit the winch which caused some damage to the radiator and headlamp. When the car arrived home I almost cried when I saw the state it was in – a far cry from when it left, looking pristine. It was some years later that I learned that my car had been used as the 'unit hack,' with anyone being allowed to drive it down to the village whenever someone needed something from the shop.

I suppose the most serious mishap occurred when the Austin was required to be part of a funeral cortège on *The Charmer*, which starred Nigel Havers. The location was a quiet street in Surbiton, and to get there meant motoring along the Kingston bypass. The Austin had been going along very well until, that is, we were within half a mile from the location, when a rather sudden and loud clattering noise coming from under the bonnet suggested that I may have a serious problem with the engine. Sure enough, on examination I found that a conrod had snapped, near to the piston, and effectively put the engine out of action. Fortunately, the conrod had bent over double and remained inside the cylinder, otherwise it could have caused a far more serious problem (if it had come though the block or crankcase).

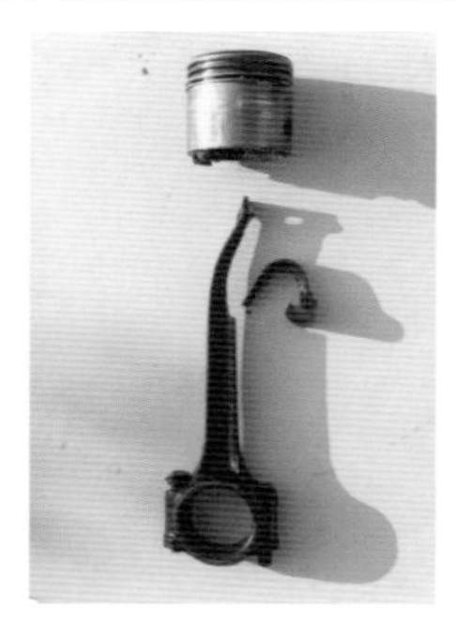

A broken conrod occurred whilst driving to the filming location for *The Charmer*.

As luck would have it, I spotted a London Weekend Television lorry approaching, and flagged it down. The driver listened to my tale of woe, and soon had the car hitched up behind his lorry on a length of strong rope. The production team was very understanding, and the Austin still played a part, just parked at the side of the road to block a modern car that may otherwise have been in shot. The journey home was at the end of a tow rope, only this time behind a 1928 Rolls-Royce, which was also part of the cortège.

On *Hercule Poirot's Christmas* the Austin decided to behave itself, but on the way home I felt that I was losing power from the engine. On this occasion I telephoned the RAC for assistance, but whilst awaiting its arrival I took a look under the bonnet, only to discover that a fastening that held the accelerator linkage to the carburettor had become loose: easily rectified with the aid of an adjustable spanner. The RAC engineer double-checked my work and, just to make sure, followed me almost to where I lived just in case further assistance was required.

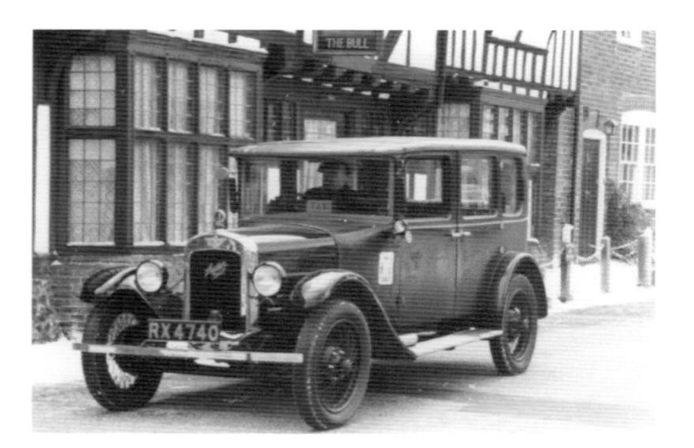

Appearing as a provincial taxi, outside the Bull Hotel (an antique shop in reality) in the Kent Village of Chilham during filming for *Hercule Poirot's Christmas*.

Hercule Poirot (David Suchet) and Inspector Japp (Philip Jackson) ready for the final shots of *Hercule Poirot's Christmas*. The cameraman was on the floor between the two front seats.

It was during the making of another episode of *Poirot*, titled *Hickory, Dickory, Dock*, that fate was to play a significant part in ensuring that matters did not go according to plan. Because of the distance involved in getting to the location – the Brompton Cemetery in Fulham where the Austin was, once again, to be part of a funeral cortège – I requested that the car be taken there on a trailer.

The Austin was required to be at the location at 07:00, so needed to be collected by 05:00 at the very latest if we were to avoid getting caught up in London-bound traffic on the A2/M2. By 05:30, the transport had still not arrived, and when it eventually turned up (at around 05:45) it was a two-wheeled trailer pulled by a rather small Ford Escort saloon car. The reason for the delay was explained as having "run out of petrol," which did not bode well for the professionalism of the driver.

The trailer was fitted with an electric winch powered by a separate battery, but when the driver came to use it, he found that it was flat, so I just drove the Austin onto the trailer and helped with securing it for the long journey. By 06:00 we were on our way; now an hour behind schedule. During the course of conversation with the driver it transpired that he did not usually transport vehicles on a trailer for a living, as he normally taught people to play the clarinet, and was actually doing this job on behalf of his brother who, in turn, was doing it as a favour for the owner of the transport company, who was 'otherwise occupied.'

I advised the driver to try and avoid the South Circular Road, as this was a notoriously congested route into London, so he took the next turning onto the A20 which went past Kidbrook Railway Station. If all went well, this would bring us back onto the South Circular further on, avoiding any congestion.

The first we knew about the road width restriction obstacles – that Lewisham Council had installed to prevent this route being used as a short cut for heavy goods vehicles – was when we found that the trailer needed to be very gently squeezed between the bollards with not an inch to spare each side. With that problem overcome, we continued until we found another pair of obstacles to impede our progress – only this time, the width between the two bollards was just that little bit narrower: halfway through, the trailer became well and truly stuck.

The car went through, but the trailer became well and truly stuck.

There was, of course, a fair amount of traffic using this road, and soon a line of delayed vehicles could be seen stretching far into the distance behind. One helpful motorist did come to review the situation and, after some deliberation, told us that, yes, we were stuck. After some time and effort (and much to the relief of those caught up in the resulting traffic jam), we did manage to reverse both car and trailer out from between the bollards. However, we noticed that, in doing so, the nearside tyre on the trailer had burst, and was now sitting there on the roadway like a dead wellington boot. The time, I noted, was now 06:45.

The driver advised me that he did have a spare wheel for the trailer, and so we jacked it up using the wheel brace from the Ford Escort, which, as luck would have it fitted the nuts on the trailer wheel. We soon had the wheel off but, on removing the spare wheel from the boot of the car, found that it was devoid of the one thing which would have made it usable: Air! The driver unhitched the trailer from the car and drove off to find a garage where the tyre could be reinflated (only to return several minutes later to collect the wheel that he had forgotten to put back in the boot).

When he did eventually return, it was quite obvious why the tyre on the spare wheel had been flat in the first place: there was a loud hissing sound coming from it as he offered it up to be fitted to the trailer. At this point I flagged down a police van which was going in the opposite direction, as I thought perhaps he may have a key which would open the emergency gate, thus allowing us to drive through and be on our way. However, he told me that the council only gave keys to council workers, the fire brigade, and the ambulance service, but not to the police. It was then that I suggested that, if he were to turn a blind eye, we could drive the rig up onto the pavement and bypass the gate and the obstacles. Thankfully, he agreed and, with tyre still hissing, we were on our way again.

Our next stop was Kwik-Fit tyres at Catford. They did not open until 08:30, but as we did not have very long to wait, we sat just outside until they opened. The rig did however attract the attention of the local traffic warden who wanted to know why we were parked on her double yellow lines. A quick look at the now totally deflated trailer tyre (plus a few words from me) saw her depart without taking any further action.

By 08:40 we were on our way again, and arrived at the location just under an hour later without any further mishap (except having caught almost every red traffic light en-route).

Fortunately for me, the film crew were otherwise occupied with interior shots, and had not noticed that one of their action vehicles had not arrived

Ready to appear in shot!

by the time requested. Alongside my 1929 Austin Sixteen, the other cars being used to form the funeral cortège were:

- A 1934 Rolls-Royce hearse
- A late 1920s Rolls-Royce saloon
- A 1934 Austin 16/6 saloon

Moving into shot behind the Rolls-Royce (but with help from behind).

All went well, except for the fact that I noticed the battery making rather heavy work of turning the engine over. Eventually, and just when we were going for a 'take' the battery decided that it had had enough, and rather appropriately, seeing as where we were, died!

The Austin was helped into shot by several members of the film crew, pushing it along behind the Rolls-Royce The resulting scene in this episode looked perfectly normal, with no sign of anyone pushing the car into shot. So, all in all, it had been quite an eventful day working on *Hickory, Dickory, Dock.*

It has to be said that I no longer hire my Austin out to film or television production companies.

Appropriately, seeing where we were, the battery 'died' and we had to be pushed into shot.

Comedian Jimmy Jewel and the late Linda Bellingham sitting comfortably in the back of the 16/6. Taken during a break in the filming of *Funny Man*, one production where the Austin behaved itself!

Chapter 13

Sergeant Murphy – a racing Twenty

Even before the cessation of hostilities in 1918, Herbert Austin was preparing for the postwar market, regarding what the motoring public may wish to purchase. He recognised that the days when motor cars were mainly chauffeur-driven were now over, and that, in future, cars were more likely to be driven by their owners.

Impressed with Henry Ford's 'one model policy,' his 20 horsepower Model T, and the Hudson Super-Six – one of which Austin personally used throughout the war – he decided that this was the best way forward for his Company, and thus concentrated on the four-cylinder Austin Twenty, developed two years before war had broken out.

The Austin Twenty, which became available to the public early in 1919, was marketed as a good all-round touring motor car, with a guaranteed top speed of seventy miles per hour – a quite unheard of boast in those days, one that the Company was prepared to back up with a written guarantee.

A postwar advert for the Austin 20/4.

A page from the 1920 Austin 20/4 catalogue and a newspaper advertisement for the same car exhibited on Stand 54 at the 1920 Motor Show states: "The dawn of 1920 will see many a practical demonstration of the favours which the 'Austin Twenty' has found with the motoring public."

In 1920, an aspiring young racing driver by the name of Felix Scriven travelled down to London from his native Yorkshire to see what new motor cars were available at the Motor Show that was being held at Olympia. After reviewing the best that Britain had to offer, he visited stand no 54 which was allocated to the Austin Motor Company. Scriven was so impressed with the Austin Twenty which was there on display (and also the Company's claim that the 'Sports' version would achieve a guaranteed 70mph), that he immediately placed an order for one. However Felix felt that, with a few minor modifications, the Austin Twenty could perhaps be persuaded to go even faster than that guaranteed by the Austin Motor Company.

Before his chassis was fully in production he asked for a few modifications to be carried out, although Austin was reluctant to do so, he eventually agreed for them to be incorporated, but only on condition that the 70mph guarantee was withdrawn.

The modifications comprised of fitting connecting rods and pistons of 95x127mm to the engine (which had been carefully balanced before assembly). The back axle ratio was raised from 3.93:1 to 3.19:1 and that Rudge wheels were fitted all round with 820x120 Palmer covers. Once delivered, Felix even tried fitting twin carburettors, but this idea was abandoned as it did not add much to the car's performance, so he reverted to the original single Claudel Hobson carburettor. The fuel used was aviation spirit and the engine was lubricated using Castrol R engine oil. The body fitted to the car was to be made slightly narrower than the normal sports tourer version, and to be of lighter construction.

When the car was ready, it was painted pillar-box red and initially named '*Felix the Cat*' after the famous cartoon character – it even sported a bronze mascot of its namesake on the radiator cap. Proudly carrying the number '15,' Scriven then set off south from Yorkshire to Weybridge, where he had entered the car in the second and sixth races of the Brooklands Easter event on 28th March 1921.

The second race was the 12th 75mph short handicap, where, being the 'limit car' he was given a start of 1 minute, 14 seconds. The distance raced was over two laps covering 5.75 miles, where the Austin averaged 70.56mph on the first lap, and 75.30mph on the second. Scriven won the 75 short race, beating the ACs of Messrs Hawker and Noble, who, annoyed at their placing, demanded a steward's enquiry, as they felt Scriven's engine dimensions could not have been listed correctly on the entry form. Scriven was equally annoyed, and insisted that the cylinder head be removed there and then in order for the dimensions to be verified. Honour duly satisfied – and since coming third in his second race (the event's sixth), where he attained an average speed of 83.5mph – the engine was reassembled and he drove back home to Bradford.

Felix Scriven's success with his Twenty did not go unnoticed back at Longbridge, and very soon Herbert Austin authorised a Works Twenty to be produced, utilising many of Scriven's ideas and modifications. This car was painted black and fitted with a distinctive white radiator shell, and given the name 'Black Maria.'

In the May of that year Scriven was to race against Black Maria. However, he failed to start and the race was won by the Austin Works car driven by Herbert Austin's son-in-law, Captain Arthur Waite (who achieved an average of 86.92mph during the second lap). In the first race on June 25th, Scriven appeared to drive very slowly, and although Arthur Waite managed to achieve 91.38mph, neither car was placed. Throughout the remainder of 1921 and into 1922, Scriven and Captain Waite (who's wife, Irene, also entered cars) fought it out for supremacy on the Brooklands track.

Longbridge test driver Lew Kings at the wheel of Black Maria (left) and Felix Scriven in Sergeant Murphy (right). Photographed at Brooklands on 24th April 1924. (Courtesy VAR archive)

At the 1922 Whitsun event at Brooklands, Felix the Cat did not excel itself, but, in subsequent races throughout that year, its performance gradually improved until, at the long handicap event held in the August, Scriven came first, having reached 90mph.

Felix entered the Twenty in the Essex Club's long handicap again in the May of 1923, but was very late in arriving at the event, and found that the competitors had already assembled in the paddock, lined up ready to start. Felix quickly dropped off his passenger, threw out the two spare wheels, and joined the other competitors – just making it in time for him to be able to compete. He achieved second place.

It was in 1924 that Felix decided to change the name of the car to 'Sergeant Murphy' after a race horse, owned at that time by a Mrs Sanford, which won the 1923 Grand National at Aintree as a rank outsider – 100:6 – and then continued to astound punters by winning almost every race in which it was entered, even when well past the time when it should have been retired. The name Sergeant Murphy first appeared in the BARC (British Automobile Racing Club) records during 1925.

In order to gain more speed, Scriven put a Laystall crankshaft into the engine, and changed the camshaft to one which had been developed by Archie Frazer-Nash. The tyre sizes were increased to 880x120 in order to get every ounce of speed out of this amazing Austin.

The bodywork on Sergeant Murphy was the four-seater tourer with which it was supplied, but later he fitted a cowled radiator, and placed decking over the two rear seats. He also added a streamline tail with two detachable wheels fitted with Palmer racing tyres, which were mounted each side. This assembly was detachable and, crated up, would be sent on ahead to his hotel in Weybridge by rail. By doing this he could accommodate three passengers and two extra spare wheels on his journey south from Yorkshire. The colour in which it appeared largely depended upon a whim and availability of paint.

Sergeant Murphy's last Brooklands win was at the 1925 Whitsun meeting when, driven by Felix, it finished first in the 90mph short handicap at 87.71mph. The Austin was also very successful in trials such as the 300 mile two day 'sealed bonnet' event organised by the *Daily Dispatch* newspaper which took place in the West Yorkshire Village of Hebden Bridge.

In spite of all the wins attributed to Felix Scriven and the undoubted success of the Austin Twenty, he was surprised that *Motor Sport Magazine* had not mentioned his wins at Brooklands in an article on Austin Racers, so in 1928 he wrote to them stating:

> Sir,
> With reference to your article, Great Racing Marques – Austin, I have perused with great interest, but was, to say the least of it, somewhat surprised that no mention was made of the 20hp Austin which I regularly raced for some six years at Brooklands.
>
> In the first place, at the Motor Show in 1920 I ordered an Austin 20 chassis which the Austin Motor Company guaranteed would be capable of 70mph.
> Before this particular chassis was put into production, I requested them to

Felix Scriven in a 'streamlined' Sergeant Murphy at Brooklands in 1925. (Courtesy Mike Worthington-Williams)

build the car exactly to my requirements. This, (after considerable discussion) they eventually agreed to do, but in view of my specification submitted they unconditionally withdrew any guarantee of speed and this I willingly risked. To cut a long story short, instead of doing 70mph the car attained 85mph. The success of the specification was so obvious to the Austin Motor Company, that they immediately proceeded to produce it as a standardised sports model.

Yours etc. Felix Scriven

Now in retirement, devoid of its racing trim and looking for a buyer. (Courtesy Mike Worthington-Williams)

Still retaining its twin rear wheels, Sergeant Murphy in 'Mufti.' (Courtesy Mike Worthington-Williams)

During its heyday at Brooklands, Sergeant Murphy was credited with being the fastest Austin Twenty ever made with a recorded lap speed of 94.99mph.

By 1926 Sergeant Murphy in 'Mufti' was pensioned off and offered for sale at £295, but sadly there were to be no buyers and after a short period 'on approval' with the Rees Brothers of Carmarthen, the car was finally sold in 1928 to a Bradford car-breaker for just £18, and was scrapped a couple of years later.

Even after parting with Sergeant Murphy, Felix continued his quest to drive as fast as it was possible to, and decided to build a special based on a Vauxhall 30/98, but employing a two litre six-cylinder Sage engine which was originally designed back in 1919 for aircraft use. However, this engine did not prove to be entirely satisfactory and after seeking advice from Parry Thomas settled on an engine supplied by him which came from his single-seater Parry Thomas Special. This, he named 'No, No Nanette.'

No, No Nanette had to be completely re-built following a devastating fire which occurred when the petrol tank collapsed and ignited the fuel whilst he was driving through Bawtry on his way to Brooklands. Soon the car was engulfed in flames which shot over 30 feet into the air, but when they started to come into the cockpit he decided that he had no alternative but to get out, and drove the car into a ditch and made good his escape as quickly as he could.

Felix Scriven died from natural causes in 1958, aged 73.

The photograph below is of a 1921 Austin 20/4 identical to Felix Scriven's Austin, the *Felix the Cat* radiator mascot is the actual mascot which was given to the owner by a member of the Scriven family.

Not Segeant Murphy or Felix the Cat but a 1921 Austin 20/4 identical to Felix Scriven's Austin. The *Felix the Cat* radiator cap mascot is however the actual one which was fitted to Scriven's car. (Courtesy Anthony Smallbone)

Chapter 14

Number 45

Number 45 was so called as it happened to be the 45th Austin motor car to be manufactured at Longbridge. It was a 25/30 horse power, chain driven, open touring car, weighing 1 ton, 16cwt, 2qrs and 17lbs, and it emerged from the Works during the latter part of 1907.

It has to be said that, at that time, there was nothing particularly remarkable about Number 45, but for some reason Herbert Austin, wearing his trademark bowler hat, chose to have his photograph taken whilst sitting at the wheel of it.

After leaving Longbridge, Number 45 was shipped over to South Africa and delivered to the Austin dealership of Messrs H Gill & Co who, for the first six months, used it as a demonstrator.

Herbert Austin at the wheel of 'Number 45.' (Courtesy *Austin Advocate* magazine)

During that time it was spotted by the Johannesburg Police authorities, who decided to purchase it for their own use. There it undertook something in excess of two thousand miles of trekking over all manner of terrain.

The driver allocated to Number 45 was Sergeant A W Ramsay of the South African Police, who recalls that the Austin was driven through the bushveld, deserts, and rivers (where the water came up over the driver's feet), and over roads which were strewn with rocks. On one occasion, in order for him to start the engine, he found it necessary to jack up the front wheels to allow the starting handle to be engaged, owing to the fact that the chassis had become twisted. Such was the flexibility of the chassis frame that, once back on a level surface, the frame returned to its normal shape.

Number 45 in service with the Johannesburg Police, exactly as received from Longbridge. (Courtesy *Austin Advocate* magazine)

On another occasion, the driver hit a tree stump and bent the trackrod, causing the front wheels to open out, but, instead of removing the bent rod and having it repaired properly, he attached one end of a stout rope to it and the other end to a tree, then gently reversed the car which then pulled the trackrod straight again.

It was, perhaps, to be expected that driving any car under such conditions would have taken a toll on its structure and, although the problems encountered were surprisingly few, it is probably worth noting that, upon investigating why the squares on the cardan shaft had worn away at the corners, it was found that the differential had become misaligned. Another minor problem was that the springs on the rocker arms broke, and an adjustment of the tappet rods was required. Over a period of ten years of hard driving, these only minor problems spoke well of the quality of Austin motor cars.

The only other items which needed attention during its life with the Johannesburg Police were the fitting of four new sets of driving chains, a new petrol tank and carburettor which were made necessary when it was transformed into an ambulance, and later, into a prison van.

Whilst with the Johannesburg Police, Number 45 carried many important people whose names became well known in connection with South Africa, such as General Louis Botha (the Prime Minister), and General Jan Smuts. Royalty, too, and members of Parliament were also conveyed in this remarkable motor car. On the occasion of The Duke of Connaught's visit to South Africa to lay the foundation stones of the Union Buildings of Pretoria, and also the Johannesburg Town Hall, Number 45 acted as pilot car.

When the Maritz Rebellion broke out on 15th September 1914, the Commissioner of Police decided that Number 45 would be far more useful as a Black Maria, and so the touring body with which it left Longbridge was removed. But, before it could be replaced with that of a police van, a further decision was taken to fit it out as an ambulance instead.

The ambulance was fitted with four stretchers, assigned for use by General Botha's staff, and was deployed throughout the entire period during which the rebellion took place, advancing almost as far as Upington on the German South-West African border. It was here that General Manie Maritz, the commander of the military camp, had assembled a sizable force of Boers prepared to rebel against the government's

Number 45 on the occasion of the Duke of Connaught's visit. (Courtesy VAR archive)

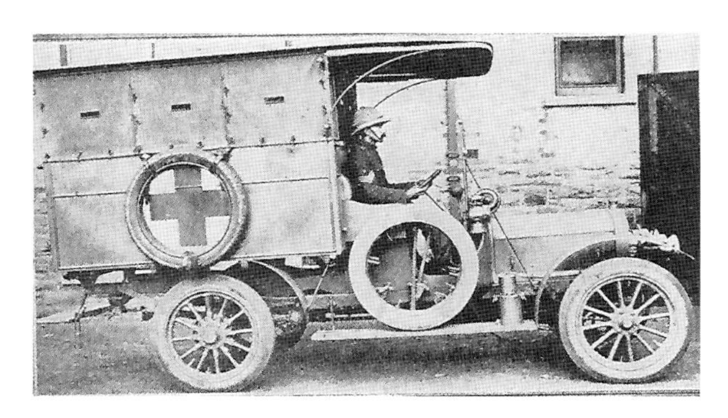

Now serving with General Botha's staff on the German South West African border, with Sergeant Ramsay at the wheel. (Courtesy *Austin Advocate* magazine)

decision to invade German South West Africa on behalf of the British government. Although officially defeated by 12th November, General Maritz fought on until 2nd February. Maritz, a German general, fled across the border into German South West Africa where he was able to take refuge.

Once the rebellion was over, Number 45 returned to Johannesburg. It was at this point that the driver, Sergeant Ramsay, left his vehicle and, acting as chauffeur to General Botha's Chief of Staff, went across into German South West Africa (which, by then, was no longer German). However, that assignment was not to last long, and soon Sergeant Ramsay was back in Johannesburg and, once again, behind the wheel of Number 45 – but this time it was a Black Maria.

What eventually became of Number 45, we shall probably never know but it is known that after the war, it was still giving good service with the Johannesburg Police Department and probably carried on doing so for some considerable time.

Now a Black Maria police van.
(Courtesy *Austin Advocate* magazine)

This advertisement from the Austin Motor Company extolling the virtues of Austin Motor Cars may actually have been published before they purchased Number 45.

Chapter 15

The rear-engined Austin

In 1923, *The Motor* magazine published an article suggesting that the motor cars currently being manufactured, should, for a number of reasons, have their engines mounted at the rear instead of at the front, whilst the drive, normally on the rear wheels, should be transferred to those at the front.

The following illustrations are of an Austin motor car that Herbert Austin had taken out a patent for a year or two prior to that article having been written.

One of the advantages that were put forward by the article in *The Motor* was that, by placing the engine at the back of the car, a chassis of any given length could provide more body space; such a configuration would lower the centre of gravity, and rear seat passengers would be situated in between the two axles, rather than over the rear axles as in conventionally designed vehicles.

The illustration suggests that the style of bodywork for which this would be most suited would have closed or semi-closed coachwork, and, with this in mind, suggests that it would ideally be used as a taxi cab.

Herbert Austin's design for a front-wheel-drive, rear-engine motor car which never made it past the drawing board. (Courtesy Bob Wyatt)

The chassis in the illustration below shows the engine mounted by three point suspension at the rear, with the flywheel at the forward end, a long propeller shaft running to the gearbox – which is built up with the differential – and final drive on the front axle; the clutch is incorporated in the flywheel, and the gearbox is rigidly attached to the chassis in more or less in the same position as that of a conventional motor car. Two universally jointed shafts extend outward from the gearbox and are attached to the two front wheels in such a manner as to allow the wheels to pivot on their steering heads, thus allowing the car to steer.

Front suspension is provided by a transverse spring, and rear suspension is provided by semi-elliptical springs, the back axle design is very similar to the typical type of front axle found in conventional vehicles, with the exception of there being no steering heads fitted.

The chassis of Herbert Austin's rear-engine motor car. (Courtesy Bob Wyatt)

For reasons which we will probably never know, the rear-engine Austin motor car was never put into production, nor was there a prototype produced by the Longbridge experimental department to assess its viability. However, we do know that a certain Austrian aircraft designer by the name of Edmond Rumpler had not only designed something along very similar lines, but had it in production by 1921. There were about 100 Rumpler Tropfenwagens manufactured, most of which saw service as taxicabs. Just two of which survive.

Chapter 16

Don't try this at home!

The photograph is of a 1928 Austin 12/4 saloon car with its front nearside wheel resting on the back of Strong Man – Mr Wilfred Briton of Leeds, who was, for reasons best known to himself, demonstrating that his body could withstand the weight of a motor car. It would be interesting to know how the front wheel was actually placed on Mr Briton's back, as there does not appear to be any evidence of a jack with which to lower the car in a controlled manner. We do know that Mr Briton survived the ordeal as Pathé filmed him demonstrating other examples of his strength a few years later, in 1939.

The Yorkshire-registered Austin weighs approximately one ton and the photograph (courtesy *Manchester Daily Mail*), was apparently taken on 13th July, 1934. What I do find puzzling was that the car was still fitted with a radiator muff in the middle of summer.

Again, I would stress, please do not try this at home!

Mr Briton with the Austin 12/4 resting on his back.

Chapter 17

"I am the only Manager around here!"

When Herbert Austin parted company with Wolseley, he invited a few of those working for him to come and work with him at his new (but then as yet to be established) motor vehicle factory. Such was their loyalty to him that they were willing to trust him at his word, and give up their jobs and follow him in his new venture.

**W A (Bobby) Howitt,
Lord Austin's Private Secretary**

One such person was William 'Bobby' Howitt, whom he engaged as his private secretary. Bobby, as he was generally known, remained Herbert Austin's private secretary from the onset of the Austin Motor Company right up until the great man died in 1941.

It was at the Austin Motor Company's Golden Jubilee celebrations in 1955 that Bobby Howitt was interviewed regarding his long association with the company, as he had been there from the very beginning he was the oldest Austin employee, with 50 years service.

He was persuaded to speak of any particular incidents which occurred during his time working for Lord Austin, and recalled an occasion when, on entering Austin's office he found him sitting at his desk reviewing the correspondence from the Company's shipping department. As Austin read the first of the letters, Bobby noticed that his eyes narrowed. On picking up the second letter and then the next he could see that Austin was becoming more and more angry as he glanced from the top of each page to the bottom.

"Who signed these letters?" he demanded. "Send him to me!" The gentleman in question was immediately sent for and quickly ushered into Austin's office.

As the man entered the office, Lord Austin looked up at the poor fellow and declared: "you have signed yourself as 'Shipping Manager.'" The man began to explain, but Austin cut him short, and threw the letters onto his desk. Then, with careful emphasis, he said "in future, please confine your signature merely to 'Shipping Section.' I am the only Manager around here!"

I suppose the gentleman in question was very fortunate that he still had a job, but then perhaps Herbert Austin, having put him in his place, considered that he had been reprimanded sufficiently, and that no further action needed to be taken.

Chapter 18

The 100hp Austins

Herbert Austin had never been afraid of testing his motor cars against those of other manufacturers, as he always had complete faith in their reliability. From as early as 1902, whilst still building up the motor car side of The Wolseley Tool & Motor Car Company, he would enter his motor cars in speed and reliability trials within the United Kingdom. Even when he left Wolseley and had established his own company, early adverts which appeared for Austin Motor cars clearly reflected the achievements of those which, though designed by him, still bore the Wolseley name.

Very shortly after the first Austins were being driven out through the gates at Longbridge, one particular customer, Oscar Thompson – having seen the success of the one which had been entered for the Scottish reliability trials, and who had previously owned a similar motor car (which, incidentally, caught fire whilst being driven over Hammersmith Bridge!) – decided that he would purchase one, which he named 'Pobble' and which went on to achieve amazing results when entered for events at the newly opened Brooklands race track.

The success of Pobble did not go unnoticed by Herbert Austin, who by the January of 1908 had set his sights on developing a motor car which he hoped would beat all others on both track and road. He set about designing and building a 100hp motor car specifically for racing and entering in the next European Grand Prix event to be held at Dieppe which, unlike those held in Great Britain, could be run on closed off public roads.

AB 983, the prototype shaft-driven 100hp Grand Prix car seen here out for a test run with Longbridge test driver Sydney Hands at the wheel. Note the tall radiator filler cap. (Courtesy VAR archive)

Probably this shaft-driven Austin's first trip out, with Austin test driver Lew Kings at the wheel. (Courtesy Austin Motor Company)

The cars were based on the six-cylinder 60hp touring chassis, the engines of which were 121mm bore x 127mm stroke. These were rebored to increase them to 127 x 127mm, where they developed 117bhp at 1500rpm. The final drive of two of the cars were by prop shaft, and the other two were chain-driven.

Although the official publication written to celebrate the Austin Motor Company's Golden Jubilee in 1955 stated that three 100hp racing cars were built, there were, in fact, four: three were there to compete and the fourth was available as a spare. The four motor cars were registered AB 983 (02/05/08), and AB 1010, AB 1011 & AB 1012 (which were all registered on 26/05/08).

The cars were first seen in public at Brooklands in May of that year, where their respective drivers – Dario Resta (No 1), John T C Moore-Brabazon (No 18), Joseph Warwick Wright (No 34), and Syd Hands as spare – were to race each other. The two chain-driven and one live axle cars were driven around two inner laps. On completion of the first lap, Dario Resta and Warwick Wright drew up together to have two of their tyres changed. John Moore-Brabazon overshot and had to reverse in order to have his tyres changed. On completion of the tyre change, Resta was first away, followed

Taken at Brooklands in May 1908, with Dario Resta at the wheel of his car, when all four cars were test driven. Note the absence of mudguards. (Courtesy VAR archive)

by Wright, and with Moore-Brabazon close behind him. Resta won the race, mainly because of a faster tyre change, taking just 3 minutes to change two rims and two tyres.

With Austin satisfied with their performance, the cars were then made ready to be transported over to Dieppe to compete in the 11th Grand Prix de l'ACF (Auto Club of France) on 7th July, 1908 – a race which consisted of 10 laps of the 47.74 mile course, making a total of 477.48 miles, all driven over public roads which started from Dieppe, and went through the villages of Envermeu, Londineres, Sept-Meules, Eu, Criel-sur-Mer, and back through Dieppe.

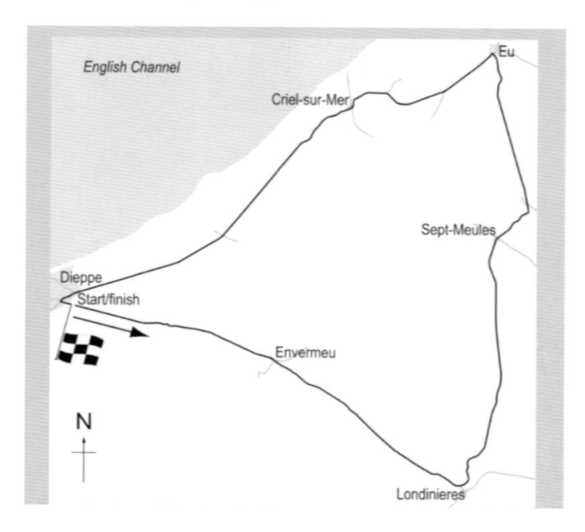

Map of the area around Dieppe where the race was held.

In order to accommodate his team of mechanics and engineers, Herbert Austin took over the entire Hotel du Cygne at Eu for the event, which amounted to 60 members from the Company.

The cars were numbered as '1,' to be driven by Resta, an Italian-American racing driver who spent almost his entire life in England; '18,' which was to be driven by Moore-Brabazon, who a year later obtained the first ever pilot's licence at Eastchurch on the Isle of Sheppey, in Kent; and '34,' which was to be driven by Warwick Wright, who went on to establish a nation-wide motor car dealership chain within the UK. There were 48 entrants, with six from England, twenty three from France, nine from Germany, six from Italy, three from Belgium, and just one from the United States of America. Each car was painted in the colours which represented their country of entry, the six cars from England were painted green to reflect the races which were previously held in Ireland, where road racing was still allowed; the French cars were blue; the 3 from Belgium, yellow; Italy's entries were red; the German cars were white; whilst the one from the United States was finished in red and white.

A couple of days prior to the race, Resta took his car around the course in order to familiarise himself with its twists, cambers, and sharp bends, he obtained remarkable speeds as he extracted every ounce of power out of the engine. Unfortunately, this resulted in him driving up an embankment when he swerved to avoid colliding with a horse-

John Moore-Brabazon at Dieppe in number 18 (AB 1010).

drawn cart, which just happened to be travelling on the wrong side of the road. The car was damaged to such an extent that he took over the spare car (AB 983), but ended up wrecking that, too, when he crashed it into some trees avoiding yet another horse-drawn cart. The Austin overturned and trapped both him and his mechanic, who was rendered unconscious. Following a near riot caused by the locals who were protesting about the accident, the local gendarmerie were summoned and considered the matter serious enough to place Resta under arrest in Dieppe Prison.

The team lined up for a photograph prior to the Grand Prix at Dieppe. Warwick Wright in number 34, J T C Moore-Brabazon in number 18 and Dario Resta in number 1.

However, both he and his mechanic were lucky – just a few days before, a British driver named Ernest Hall-Watt was killed whilst testing his Renault around the circuit, and on the same day another driver managed to run into and kill a spectator, so it is little wonder that the locals were not all that enthusiastic about the forthcoming race.

On hearing of the incident and the resulting incarceration of one of his drivers, Austin immediately set about securing Resta's release in time for him to participate in the Grand Prix. The two crashed cars were frantically rebuilt into one by the engineers which Austin had thoughtfully brought over from England and, with additional parts having been rushed over from Longbridge, they completed the job in time for the race.

The race commenced at 06:00 to ensure that even the slowest cars could at least finish whilst it was still light. Dario Resta in '1' took to the track first, followed one minute later by Willy Pöge ('2') in a Mercedes. Moore-Brabazon and Warwick Wright started 18th and 34th respectively.

The Austins driven by Resta and Moore-Brabazon ran well but were soon outclassed by their rivals. Their progress was not helped by both having to stop several times to change tyres, with Resta requiring ten replacement covers!

The race was won by the German driver Christian Lautenschlager in his 140hp Mercedes, which averaged 69mph over the entire course. Moore-Brabazon finished 18th at 54.8mph taking 8 hours 42 minutes and 50 seconds, and Resta came 19th taking 8 hours, 46 minutes and 50 seconds, both setting an average speed of 50mph. Warwick Wright retired due to engine failure after completing just four laps. His mechanic was blamed for failing to ensure that the engine had sufficient oil in the sump.

In this interesting French postcard we see the three drivers of the 100hp Austins at the wheel of one of the shaft-driven vehicles, but looking first at the bottom car we see Warwick Wright (not 'Wrigth'), but then look at the one in the top right hand corner, yes, it's the same car but the negative has been reversed, as the gearlever and handbrake now appear to be in the wrong place. The one shown top left is again the same car.

Out of the 47 cars entered for the race only 23 managed to complete the course. France, the host country, had entered twenty three cars and quite expected to come out on top but, regrettably for them, this was not to happen, and as a result there were no Grand Prix events held on French soil for another 4 years.

On their return to England, Herbert Austin personally presented each of the drivers with a small silver cup, as a 'thank you.' The cars went back to the Works where they each received a complete overhaul. The car that was assembled from the spare and Dario Resta's car was taken apart, and rebuilt as two separate cars again – which leads one to believe that, in truth, they were not all that badly damaged.

All the cars had their racing bodywork removed and replaced with smart touring coachwork, and two of them with Vitesse Phaeton coachwork, these were purchased by Henry Garner, a Birmingham Austin agent and dealer where they were to be sold on.

The car driven by Moore-Brabazon (AB 1010) was sold on to Sir Francis Hickman Bacon, Bt. of Thonnock Hall, Lincolnshire. Sir Francis reregistered the car 'BE 3,' a number which he transferred from an earlier car that he had owned, and the Austin was used regularly by him right up until his death in 1929. The car was supplied to him fitted with a four-seater Roi de Belge touring body and it also came with an additional two-seater body, which was also made for him by Austin. During his lifetime, Sir Francis was frequently seen behind the wheel of this car, driving around the roads in the Gainsborough area of Lincolnshire.

After Sir Francis' death, the car was handed back to the Austin Motor Company to add to its collection of early motor cars. On receiving BE 3 and realising its significance, the Company set about replacing the coachwork with a replica of how the car would have appeared for the Dieppe Grand Prix. A task which was, in all probability, assigned to the coachbuilding apprentices, and is certainly the bodywork in which BE 3 appears today.

One of the prop-driven 100hp Austins with a Vitesse Phaeton touring body that was sold to a prominent member of the Stock Exchange through Henry Garner, the Birmingham car dealer. (From the April 1912 edition of *Austin Advocate* magazine)

Another one of the 100hp Austins. This one chain-driven, andfitted with smart Vitesse Phaeton coachwork. One feature being that the seat beside the driver tilts sideways to allow access to the seats behind.

Dario Resta actually owned his car and was therefore free to advertise it for sale. The advertisement printed in *The Autocar* magazine of 12th September 1908 read:
"Austin 1908 Grand Prix racer. RAC Rating 59.6hp, just converted to touring chassis, immediate delivery at makers' works. £750. D Resta. Park Lodge, Bath Road, Reading."

One person interested in buying it was the world heavyweight boxer Jack Arthur Johnson, who took AB 1012 for a test drive, but in the end did not purchase it, probably due to it having been built from the two cars involved in crashes whilst in Dieppe. It was

World heavyweight champion boxer Jack Johnson seated in his replica 100hp Austin.

taxed on 25th November, 1908, so it must have been sold and used subsequent to that. Johnson did, however, purchase a very similar motor car directly from Longbridge a couple of years later. This was built on a shaft-driven 60hp chassis fitted with the 60hp engine, and with bodywork similar to that fitted to the Grand Prix Cars. The car was registered in London between April 1910 and July 1911 as LA 7701.

AB 983 (the shaft-driven spare) was fitted with a very smart two seater coach-built body and was purchased by Mr H G Evans of the Manor House, Tettenhall, Wolverhampton.

World heavyweight boxer Jack Johnson at the wheel of his six-cylinder Locomobile. He raced against American Racing Ace, Barney Oldfield at the Sheepshead Track on New York's Long Island on 28th October 1910. Oldfield won the race with his six-cylinder Knox. It is often wrongly stated that the car driven by Johnson was one of the 100hp Austins.

The spare car, which helped Dario Resta compete in the Grand Prix, now rebuilt as a smart, two-seater touring car.

The only known survivor out of the four cars is BE 3 which is on permanent display at the British Motor Museum, Gaydon.

Reg no	Drive	Driver	Race no	Coachwork prior to being sold	Sold to	Fate
AB 1010	Chain	Moore-Brabazum	18	Roi des Belge	Sir Francis Hickham-Bacon	BE 3 Gaydon Museum
AB 1011	Chain	Wright	34	Vitesse	H Garner (Agent)	Unknown
AB 1012	Shaft	Resta	1	Vitesse	H Garner (Agent)	Unknown
AB 953	Shaft	S. Hands	(Spare)	2-seater	H G Evans	Unknown

BE 3 after having a replica Grand Prix style body fitted following its return to Longbridge in 1929 ...

... and as it appears today at Gaydon. Note that the rear end is quite different to the Austin as raced. It is interesting that, whilst the car was raced in green, it should now be represented in red; Italy raced in red.

Chapter 19

Taking a Swift look at the first Austin Seven

One would certainly be forgiven for believing that the first Austin Seven motor car was manufactured in 1922, for indeed that was the year when Herbert Austin's world famous 'baby' Austin went on to sell 290,000 world-wide over a period of eight years. The earlier Seven was first released for sale to the motoring public at the London Motor Show in 1909, just three years after the formation of the Austin Motor Company.

The 1910 Austin Seven on the left and the Swift version on the right. (Courtesy of The Swallow Owner's club)

The Austin in question was described as a voiturette. It had just two seats, a single cylinder engine (developed from the block of the 18/24 engine), and rated at just under seven horsepower (6.8 to be precise). It was offered for sale at just £150, and was aimed in particular to the young or the 'lady' drivers. The Seven was designed by Austin and the first prototype was manufactured at Longbridge. But, because there were still only limited production facilities available at the Longbridge factory, for it to be manufactured in any quantity, Harvey Du Cros (one of Herbert Austin's financial backers), arranged for full production to be transferred to the Swift Motor car factory in Coventry, in which he also had financial interests.

Harvey Du Cros arranged for the drawings, and such patterns as were necessary, to be transferred over to the Swift factory, where, under the control of R H Every, the little cars were put into production alongside a seven horsepower Swift voiturette. Both cars were identical, and the only way a Swift could be distinguished from an Austin was by various name plates, the slight difference in the shape of the bonnet, and the badge on the radiator.

Regrettably, the little Seven did not enjoy the accolades accorded to its later namesake, and was actually not considered to be a very reliable motor car and, therefore, stayed in production for only two years. However, during that time 1030 of them were manufactured, of which 162 were badged up as Austins and 868 as Swifts. Not surprisingly, very few are known to have survived.

An advert extolling the virtues of the new Austin Seven voiturette.

An automotive journalist wrote

The Austin Seven was reviewed in *Automotive Journal* in November, 1909, in an article which gives a glowing account of "the new Austin runabout." It is interesting to note that nowhere in this account is there any mention of Swift. The review reads thus:

> "Users of small cars – and there must be a very large percentage of the motoring public who have some use for a little runabout – will turn with special interest this year to the production of the Austin factory, for they have included a new single cylinder chassis which has essentially been designed for them. It may perhaps come as a surprise that a firm like the Austin Co should have turned their attention to such small work; but that having done so should have made a particularly good job of it, and everyone acquainted with Austin practice will be willing to believe. There have been a few manufacturers who have thought it worthwhile to build a car of this type, essentially intended for sale at a moderate price, on such lines; It has, of course been specially designed for this purpose, but it has quite the Austin stamp in several respects, and great attention has been made to making the chassis thoroughly durable.

It must have been a very cold winter's day when the owner of this Scottish registered Austin Seven chose to stop for a photograph.

As a complete car it makes a very handy little vehicle, being small but very cosy, with its well-arranged two seater body, windscreen, hood, and patent leather flaps between the dashboard and the seats. Driver and passenger are thus well protected, for the body in this form is virtually enclosed.

In speaking of the special features of the chassis construction, it is difficult to select one point more than another on such a car where even the most ordinary details may have some claim to being considered uncommon because they are not usually found in such machines. The pressed steel frame, three quarter elliptic suspension, and worm and selector steering, would all be of orthodox form in larger work, but stand out as characteristics on this little model.

The live rear axle is designed very closely to Austin standard practice, and the road wheels are supported on tubular extensions of the axle casing as in big cars. There are two universal joints on the propeller-shaft; and the gearbox contains three forward speeds and a reverse, which are operated by an enclosed gate change-speed mechanism forming a reduced scale replica of that on the more powerful models. The clutch is of a leather-faced cone type and the engine has a single cylinder fitted with magneto ignition and also a supplementary battery system to facilitate starting.

The lubrication system on the engine is a copy of that on the larger models, oil being forced by a pump into the crankshaft bearings. As oil oozes out of the bearings onto the webs of the crank, it is caught by small scoops, and by the action of centrifugal force finds its way onto the big end of the connecting rod through oil-ways drilled in the crank pin. Both valves are mechanically operated and are placed side by side so that one cam-shaft can work them. The gearwheels that drive the cam-shaft and magneto spindle are fully enclosed in an extension of the crank chamber. A half compression device is fitted to facilitate starting; it is interposes a wedge under the exhaust-valve-tappet and thereby raises the valve slightly off its seat.

Cooling is effected by the thermo-siphon principle, large bore pipes connecting the upper and lower ends of the cylinder jacket with the radiator of the well-known Austin pattern.

At the rear end of the camshaft is a skew-gear for driving the vertical spindle. On the lower end of this spindle is the oil pump, whilst its upper end carries the commutator for the battery circuit. Both camshaft and crankshaft are carried direct by bearings formed in the cast iron crank chamber, and the same method of support is employed for the gear shafts, the gear box being made of cast-iron. Both engine and gearbox are carried on an underframe, which is fastened to a pair of the transverse members of the main frame.

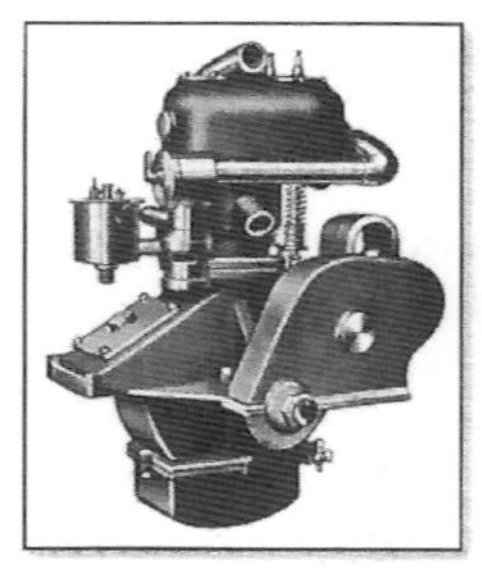

Two views of the Austin Seven's single cylinder engine.

An unusual scheme has been adopted in connection with the brake arrangement, for both the hand and foot brake operate upon the same drums on the hubs of the rear wheels. The brakes themselves are, of course separate and independent; they are compensated by wire cables, and are adjustable.

The control devices manipulated by the driver are identical to those on the larger Austin cars – an important point, especially when the driver is a novice anxious to qualify for higher powered machines. The throttle is controlled by a pedal accelerator, and has a lever above the steering wheel for setting the minimum engine speed. The ignition, however, is not hand timed.

Essentially a two-seater, the chassis is equipped and sold with a standard body, which affords comfortable accommodation for the driver and passenger, while presenting a smart and well-balanced appearance. An ingenious and simple device in the form of light curved brackets attached to the dashboard enables high patent leather flaps to be used instead of side doors between the dashboard and the driver's seat, and these do much to protect the occupants in rough weather. Fitted with a good hood and windscreen, both of which look very suitable for this little car, the finished vehicle makes as cosy a runabout as could well be desired."

An owner wrote in her diary

The following is an account; written up in the diary of a lady driver who noted down her trials and tribulations whilst owning an Austin Seven, which I suspect may have been secondhand. The motor car in question was given to her by her husband shortly after they became married, and was purchased in London whilst they were on their honeymoon.

The car remained in her ownership for just eight months, during which time it covered 2000 miles being driven mainly around the Dole, Henfield, and Brighton area where she lived. The diary commences on 3rd July 1911, the day the vehicle was purchased.

July 3rd. "Went and saw the car."
July 4th. "Alick (Brother) arrived at 11:30, went with me and got the car. Exhaust box fell off. Aunt Lottie for lunch. Left 3:15. Home 7:45. Leg ached from working clutch."
July 5th. "Alick and I went to Henfield in the car, took Mrs Wisden for a little spin."
July 6th. "Alick and I went to Brighton in the car – ran badly."
July 7th. "Drove Alick back to Ticehurst. Lunch at Cross-in-Hand, Tea, Lewis. Car ran well."
July 14th. "Percy (Husband) and I went to Worthing and Brighton in the car. Broke the windscreen and both mudguards from vibration."
July 19th. "Went to Henfield this morning. Brought Toto (Dr Fredrick Lewis) back to lunch. Drove him round to Steyning. He adjusted the magneto – much better."
July 23rd. "Mrs W and Bee Cotton came to tea. I fetched and took them back in the car. Clutch very fierce and mudguard broke again."
July 25th. "Percy and I went to Goodwood; car broke magneto carbon coming home. Came back ten miles on battery. Engine would not pull, bottom gear nearly all the way, engine boiled and leaked."
July 26th. "Powell came to mend the car, but did nothing. Men from Sussex Motor Garage came and I drove into Henfield after tea."

Side view of 1909 Austin Seven. (Courtesy Bob Wyatt)

July 27th. "Percy and I went to Eastbourne. The car went well. Home at 6 o'clock."
July 31st. "Cleaned car all morning. Took Mrs Wisden and Bunch to Hurtspierpoint and to the Chaplins, had a run in Charlie's huge De Dietrich which will do 70. He let me drive!"

(Author's note: this was not the star of the silent screen, but a local motor enthusiast who, as a member of the government (1895-6), had played a major part in drafting the Locomotive & Highways, or Emancipation Act.)

August 2nd. "Went to Brighton to fetch Mrs Bird. Car stopped through heat but I got there all right."
August 4th. "I went onto Toto's and messed about with the car there, but it was no better."
August 12th. " ... to Shoreham after tea and had tyres changed."
August 14th. " Drove Mrs Wisden and Bunch to Shoreham. They went on the beach and I had the clutch done at garage."
August 15th. "Percy and I went to Tunbridge Wells to tea with Mother – clutch no better."
August 21st. "Drive Mrs W and Bunch to Brighton – car ran badly."
Sept 1st. "Marjory and I went to Tunbridge Wells for the day – home 7:30, car overheated and broke another mudguard. Brakes bad."
Sept 3rd. "Toto came to lunch; he adjusted the carburettor and cleaned out the radiator but says clutch badly designed and will always be troublesome."
Sept 6th. "Went to Brighton after lunch, had leak in radiator mended. Car wouldn't start Crowd gathered outside Parlmeira Stores – all jostling. Exhausted from swinging engine, but home eventually."

Sept 13th. "Percy went to London by 8:30 (train). Marjory and I motored up. Car went well to Croydon then ran very badly. Had magneto seen to at Jacksons."
Sept 17th. "I drove Mrs W to (indecipherable) to tea. Brakes jammed on. Lamp bracket broke from vibration."
Sept 19th. "Had brakes mended and carrier fixed at Powell's."
Sept 20th. "I drove Mrs W to Worthing. Car went very badly – Toto mended car after tea and went so well she climbed Pycombe in Second."
Sept 22nd. "Took Percy in to see Toto. He timed my magneto. Had another broken mudguard mended."

It was here that the diary entries ceased, recording a rather sad chronicle of poor reliability of a marque whose whole reputation was built on providing owners with a reliable means of transportation. The Austin was part exchanged in early 1912 for a three year old Adler which was to provide trouble-free service until the outbreak of the Great War, when, because of it being a German car, it was not considered patriotic to be seen driving about in it.

A survivor re-visited

In 1959, one of the surviving Austin Seven voiturettes, which had become part of the Austin Motor Company's collection of early motor cars, was taken out for a road test. Norman Milne, the Company's assistant press officer together with Kevin Glover, the editor of the *Austin Magazine* were given the task of putting this little motor car through its paces for an article which was to appear in the Christmas edition of the magazine. The car was taken first to the experimental department where, under the watchful eye of George Coates, it was thoroughly prepared for its brief return to the road. The following is an account of that event written by Norman Milne:

"I recall that, despite the absence of any speedometer, we reckoned that the top speed to be about 35mph and that it cruised quite comfortably around 20-25 mph even though it was desperately sluggish in most respects. Its hill climbing ability was marginal, it wouldn't look at Rose Hill (1 in 8 maximum gradient; 1 in 5 overall average), which the 1922/23 Seven could manage at 15mph minimum: later the 'box' 1930s Seven could ascend the hill at 20mph and the later 'Rubies' at 25mph in third gear. It simply hated hills.

It could just about manage the steepest part of Kendal End between Barnt Green and the Rednal Runabout in first gear. That gradient was 1 in 12 or 1 in 12½.

Mind you, even by the standards of its day it was quite high geared at 21mph/1000rpm in top gear, so that 32mph would have been around 1500rpm. The later Sevens would have been doing more than 2200rpm. I suppose, for its day little more than a decade after the world started building motor cars, it was quite advanced and reasonably efficient. Mind you, it would have been better off with a pair of cylinders rather than just the one.

Really, from then on, all the Austin cars were great hill climbers, partly due to good torque, heavy flywheels, and often unnecessarily low-gearing, some may say due to the close proximity of Rose Hill to the Austin Works, the Austin's could leave the opposition standing when it came to ascending gradients."

Referring now to the opening paragraphs from the original instruction book supplied with every Seven:

"We have produced this small replica of our large models with the objective of providing a car suitable for beginners, and younger members of the family; also to do the work within its powers usually done by the larger and more expensive cars at greater risk and expense.

Norman Milne with a look of absolute terror on the downhill stretch of the test run.

Whilst uphill, a little extra help was required.

Before we could offer such a car to the public, we had to give the matter very serious consideration, because we realise that the purchase of such a car requires just as much reliability and freedom from expense in repair that the owner of a larger vehicle would expect.

To effect such a result we would not therefore reduce in any degree the quality of the materials or workmanship in the vital parts, but we found that by very careful designing and thorough organisation of production we should be able to produce, and sell, a small two-seated car with all the necessary features and best quality, at a very reasonable price of £150.

We decided that it was absolutely necessary to limit the seating capacity to two persons, by doing so we were enabled to reduce the weight to the lowest point without sacrificing the stability of the parts.

As the motor has only one cylinder, we have included a half compression device and coil ignition, so that the operation of starting should be as simple and easy as possible."

The car which Norman Milne road tested in 1959 (BJ 1935) still exists and may be seen in the British Motor Museum at Gaydon, Warwickshire. In total, it is believed that four 1910 registered Sevens and one registered in 1911 are still around today.

The same car currently on display at The British Motor Museum, Gaydon.

Chapter 20

Austin armoured cars for Russia – Bronyeavtomobil Ostin

By 1911, the Austin Motor Company had made significant inroads into Russia. In Russia North, the agents for Austin Motor Cars were James E Bell & Sons, who were based in Moscow, whilst in Russia South, Heinrich Schutt, of Hamburg, handled sales of Austin motor cars to customers living nearer to the German border.

As early as 1906 Austin motor cars had been exported to Russia where they were purchased by the grand dukes and other personages of note who were able to afford such luxuries, but by 1911 the Russian Military Authority were seriously considering introducing motor traction to replace horses for military purposes, and organised a reliability trial of lorries which, laden to their declared carrying capacity, were to take part in a gruelling drive from St. Petersburg (Petrograd) to Moscow, and then from Moscow to a place called Gzhel and back, and then returning to St. Petersburg, covering a total distance of 1000 miles.

The six-cylinder 50hp Austin landaulet owned by Professor C de Kronstchoff of St Petersburg who purchased it from James Bell & Sons in 1911. (Courtesy *Austin Advocate* magazine)

Lorries from six German companies, and two from England, took part and as, at that time, Austin had not commenced manufacturing such vehicles, their agents, James Bell & Sons, provided a 3-ton Halley lorry as one of the two English entries. On completion of the trial the lorries were lined up to be inspected by the Russian Emperor, Tsar Nicholas II, who declared his interest and subsequent approval of the newly formed Russian Army Automobile Corps.

It was not until two years later that the Austin Motor Company produced its first commercial vehicle, a 2/3-ton twin propshaft lorry.

Austin by now had established an enviable reputation with the quality of its Automobiles, which were considered to be very well built, reliable, and rugged enough to withstand the generally poor condition of the Russian roads, and, with careful tuning of the engines, quite capable of coping with the equally poor quality of Russian petrol. So it came as no real surprise when in the August of 1914, a delegation from the Russian Imperial Army arrived at Longbridge to discuss the purchase of a considerable quantity of vehicles to the value of £500,000 and a further £50,000 for the supply of spare parts.

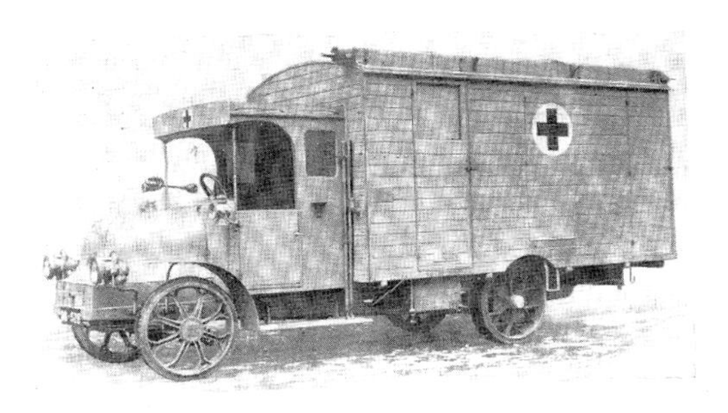

A 12-stretcher ambulance of the type ordered by the Imperial Russian Army. (Courtesy *Austin Advocate* magazine)

Three of the 2/3-ton lorries parked outside the Austin Works prior to shipment to Russia. (Courtesy *Austin Advocate* magazine)

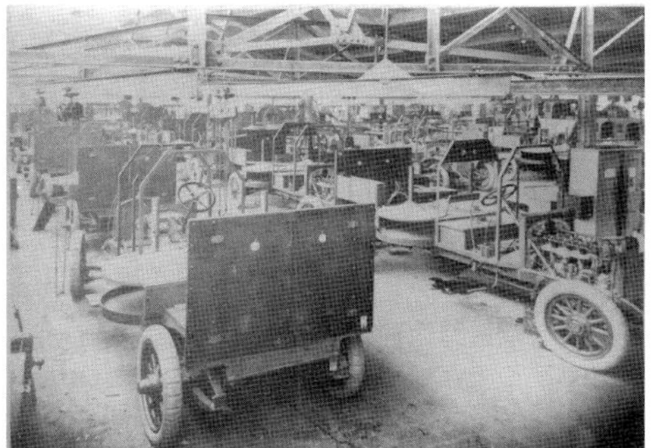

Armoured Cars (First Series) in the course of construction at Longbridge. (Courtesy VAR archive)

High on their list were 100 2/3-ton lorries – 18 to be supplied as fully equipped workshops, 16 20hp tank wagons (with divisions to contain oil, petrol and grease), eight binned spares lorries, and 20 12-stretcher ambulances. They also required a fleet of 48 armoured cars – a product which, up until then, Austin had not given any thought to manufacturing.

The Russians, however, knew exactly what they wanted with regard to the design of these vehicles, and soon outlined their requirements to the Austin design team. The first of these were to be built on the 30hp colonial chassis, have a range

This 'official' Austin publicity photograph shows the first (First Series) Armoured car to be manufactured at Longbridge. (Courtesy VAR archive)

of 150 miles on a full tank of petrol, and attain a top speed of 38mph – they could actually achieve 45mph on good roads, even though when completed they weighed in at three tons.

Each car, which cost £1150, was to accommodate a crew of four, and to be armed with a 7.62mm Maxim water-cooled machine gun in each of the turrets. The translation of Austin Armoured Cars into Russian was 'Bronyeavtomobil Ostin.'

Before the Russian delegation departed for home, they were treated to a banquet in their honour at which many of the Company's directors and their wives were invited to attend. However, being from the Imperial Russian Army, the members of the delegation arrived dressed, as they considered appropriate, in full military uniform looking for all the world like cast members from *The Student Prince.*

Another view of the first Austin (First Series) Armoured car. (Courtesy VAR archive)

The entire order, including the armoured cars which were designated Austin First Series, was completed and shipped over to St Petersburg just before the winter set in, and within three months of the order being received.

A British Army Third Series Austin mounted on the 1 1/3-ton chassis. Note the machine gun deflectors on the turrets, the search lights and the twin rear wheels. These vehicles were used by the 17th (Armoured Car) Battalion of the Tank Corps. (Courtesy VAR archive)

A 2nd series Austin destroyed possibly near Kolomyia on July 1917. Note the rear combat wheels. (Courtesy Michael Delera)

Austin of the first series cars of the 8th Auto-M.G. platoon. The first car named Sil'nyy (Strong), having the original unmodified armour, was damaged in action on 22nd February 1915 near Lomza (Poland), one of the first combat actions of the Austins. Bullet holes can be seen in the 7mm armoured turret. The 4mm hull armour below is also pierced. The car has Combat wheels. Another damaged Austin Slavnyl (Glorious) is seen in the background fitted with road wheels. (Courtesy Michael Delera)

In combat, it was found that the 3.4/4mm thick chrome-nickel armour plating fitted at Longbridge was not thick enough, and could be penetrated by machine gun bullets, so the Russians replaced it with 7mm plating that proved much better. This extra weight did restrict the vehicle's ability to be driven on anything other than decent road surfaces, as the chassis and engine was not designed to carry the additional weight of the thicker armour.

The following year the Russians placed an order for a further 50 armoured cars to be referred to as 'Austin Second Series.' These were built onto a 1⅓-ton truck chassis with 50hp engines, and were fitted with 7mm thick armour plating. Then, in August of 1916, the Russians placed yet another order for a further 60 armoured cars that were to be designated as 'Austin third series.' Based on previous combat experience, this series incorporated further improvements such as inclusion of a rear driving position to enable the car to be driven backwards, and thus provide it with greater manoeuvrability. Bulletproof glass was fitted to the driver's front vision slot, and the large side windows were replaced with narrow slots protected by a hinged flap. There was also a headlamp fitted to the top of the turrets. These were delivered between February and August of 1917.

A further order of 70 cars of this series, which were to have had a strengthened chassis and double rear wheels, was cancelled due to the political changes that occurred in October of that year. However, 40 vehicles from this order had already been built and were taken up by the British Army – 24 of them went to the Middle East, and the remaining 16 were allocated to the 17th (Armoured Car) battalion of the Tank Corps.

The Crews for this battalion were made up of men from Canada, Australia, New Zealand, South Africa, France, the USA and, of course, Great Britain. They were deployed in an area around the French/Belgium border and succeeded in destroying any chances the German Army may have had in winning the war. As it was, the Battalion lost five cars, but the remaining 11 cars fought on, taking more and more ground from the occupying forces – with their bravery mentioned three times in German dispatches. They were employed in what was to be the final battle of World War I, where they fought alongside French troops in the Battle of the Marne, with a further loss of two cars, one officer, and four other ranks.

An Austin armoured car of the third series in action with the British Army in the battle of the Marne. The Vickers Machine guns had been replaced by Hotchiss MGs. (Courtesy P Radley)

Third series Austin 1918 in use by the British Army's 17th Tank and Armoured Car Battalion. (Courtesy Michael Delera)

The Austin Motor Company built a total of 480 armoured cars, many seeing service all over the world. Some were captured and used against their rightful owners, and a few even survived to see service during the 1939-45 conflict. There is, as far as it is known, only one survivor which is housed in the Artillery Museum in St Petersburg. The vehicle in question, named 'Vrag Kapitala' ('The Capital's Enemy'), is of the Third Series, and was reputed to be the vehicle upon the bonnet of which Vladimir Lenin stood in April 1917 to address the masses. However, it was later discovered that this particular vehicle was not manufactured until the August of 1919, just over two years later.

An interesting sequel to this chapter, and reported upon in the BMC house magazine *BMC World*, was that in 1967, the annual military parade held in Moscow's Red Square (and, on this occasion, broadcast on *BBC* television news) was seen to be headed by an Austin Armoured car. This was noted by Alf Depper, who had been sent over with the first shipment of Austin lorries and armoured cars to teach the Russians how to drive and maintain them. The chairman of British Motor Holdings, George Harriman also noted its presence, and could not believe his eyes that this 1914 Longbridge product was still running, and heading this parade of Soviet Russian might. However, that particular Austin turned out to be only a mock-up, used simply to show the world how far the Soviet Union had progressed since the start of the revolution fifty years previously.

The one surviving armoured car on display at The Artillery Museum, St Petersburg.

According to Dmitry Ponarovkin, via a fax from Moscow to BMC in 1997, about 20 fake armoured cars were similarly manufactured specifically for the parade, using standard Russian motor cars as the base.

The 'mock-up' Austin armoured car seen in the 50th centenary parade. (Courtesy *BMC World*)

Chapter 21

Mr Pulitzer's 'prize' Austin Seven

In 1928 the American Millionaire, Mr Herbert (Tony) Pulitzer decided that he would very much like to own one of Herbert Austin's little seven horsepower motor cars, ostensibly for use around his Palm Beach home in Florida.

Mr Pulitzer did not want just an ordinary production Seven, but instead rather fancied a specially commissioned two-seater coupé with a 'dicky' (or 'rumble') seat. The lower part of the coachwork to be finished in faux cane appliqué.

The Maythorne Austin Seven built for Herbert Pulitzer. (*The Austin Magazine*, 1929)

Following contact with Longbridge, and no doubt Herbert Austin himself, he settled upon a rather smart version of the Seven, the coachwork for which would be contracted out to Messrs Maythorne of Biggleswade, who would normally build bodies on Rolls-Royce or Bentley motor cars.

There is no record of how pleased Mr Pulitzer was with his new purchase, but it was retained at his Palm Beach home for 52 years following his death at the age of 60 in 1957. It reappeared again in 2009 when it was to be auctioned by Bonhams, where it fetched a staggering £33,750.

The little Seven could not have been used very much whilst in his ownership, as it had only 6300 miles on the clock when submitted for auction.

And 81 years later, still looking as good as new. (Courtesy Bonhams Auctioneers)

Chapter 22

... and finally

This chapter adds a little more to two of the subjects which were featured in my previous book *An Austin Anthology*. The first concerns the 40hp 'motor home' from chapter seven, when, since the publication of that book, a significant item came to light within the pages of the weekly Scottish motoring publication, *Motor World & Industrial Vehicle Review* (22nd July, 1909), in which there appeared an account of the 40hp Austin motor home's first outing with seven specially invited guests, plus a chef on board to prepare and cook them a hot meal.

The 40hp motor home about to set off on its maiden journey to Brighton. (Courtesy *Motor World & Industrial Vehicle Review*)

Starting off at 11am from the Motoring Club in Coventry Street, West London, their route took them down to Brighton, via Westminster, Brixton, Reigate, Horley & Crawley, where they stopped at The George Hotel before continuing on to Brighton.

The report tells of how the vehicle made almost the entire journey of 100 miles in top gear, travelling at an average speed of 20mph, and that when it reached Brighton and was parked up on the sea front it 'attracted considerable interest' from people who were keen to see such an unusual vehicle.

The report did mention that the entire journey took three hours to complete, but it did not say whether this included the stop at The George. Which, no doubt would have included a drink or two as well as being seen as a 'comfort stop'!

On the return journey to London, somewhere between Brighton and Horley. they all enjoyed a cooked meal. The very first time (according to the report) that a cooked meal had been prepared, served and eaten in a fast moving motor vehicle.

The 40 hp Austin motor home taken on its inaugural journey in July 1909. Travelling in the vehicle (L to R), were Charles Pinnock, Charles Jarrott, Walter du Cros, D' Arcy Baker, WA Turpin, Harvey du Cros Jnr, Eustace Gray, and the chef. (Courtesy *Motor World & Industrial Vehicle Review*)

The second 'discovery,' which appeared in the same journal, concerns the 35hp motor car known as 'Pobble' (V 33) owned by Oscar Thompson. Here we see this famous motor car in its original form entered in the Shelsley Walsh hillclimb of 1909 where, on this occasion, it was driven by the Austin test driver Syd Hands. There was no mention of Oscar Thompson, the owner of the car, who it is understood drove Pobble in a subsequent trial on the same day (see chapter four of *An Austin Anthology*).

'Pobble' driven at speed at Shelsley Walsh hillclimb. (Courtesy *Motor World & Industrial Vehicle Review*)

Looking for the first book? *An Austin Anthology* is available fom Veloce:

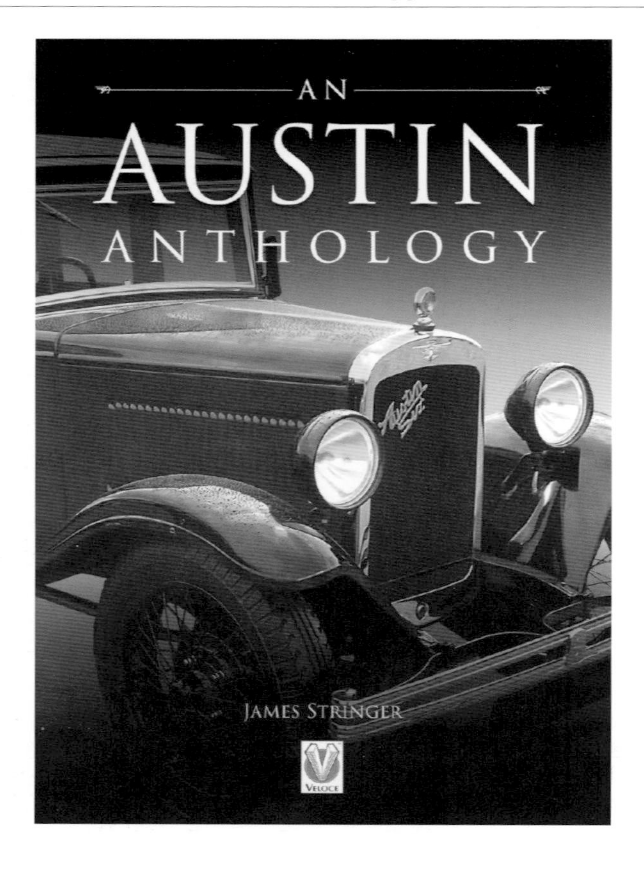

An engaging collection of short stories featuring some of the more unusual products that came out of Longbridge, such as the 40hp motor car, probably the first motor home ever built, and the biplane small enough to keep in your garage.

ISBN: 978-1-787111-91-2
Hardback • 21x14.8cm • 112 pages • 109 pictures

For more information and price details, visit our website at www.veloce.co.uk • email: info@veloce.co.uk • Tel: +44(0)1305 260068

Immortal Austin Seven tells the story of this most popular of prewar cars in all its variations, from the earliest Chummy of the 1920s through Sports, Military, Box and Ruby Saloons to the exquisite Twin Cam racers of the late 1930s. The book includes period, detail drawings and rarely seen photographs – a must for the Austin Seven enthusiast.

ISBN: 978-1-845849-79-5
Hardback • 24.8x24.8cm • 228 pages • 319 pictures

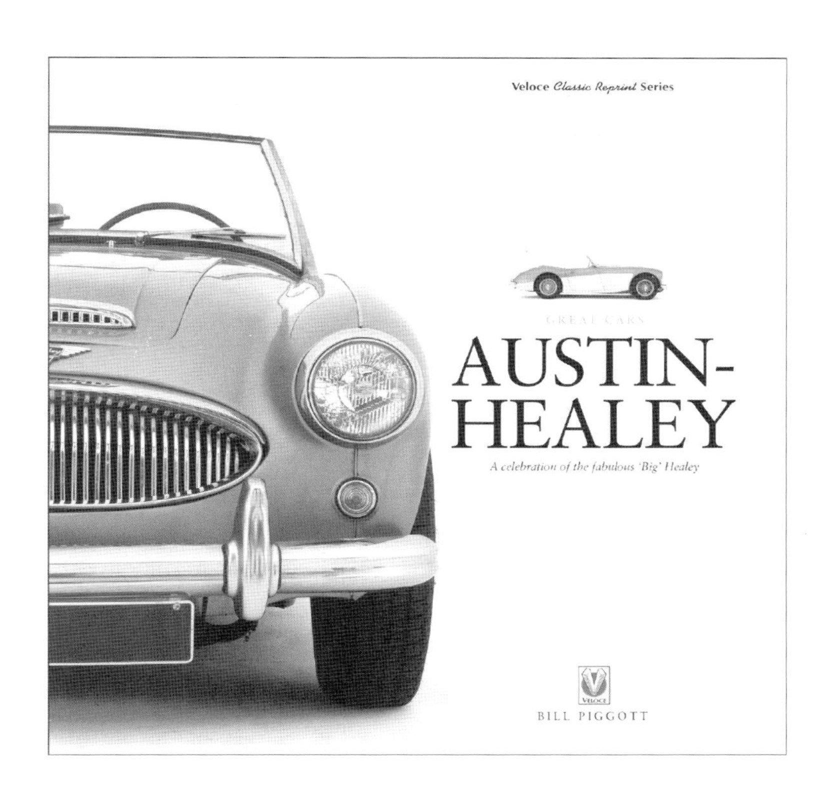
Veloce Classic Reprint Series
AUSTIN-
HEALEY
A celebration of the fabulous 'Big' Healey
BILL PIGGOTT

INDEX